Directory of African
Film-Makers and Films

Directory of African Film-Makers and Films

Compiled and edited by Keith Shiri

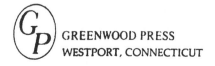

GREENWOOD PRESS
WESTPORT, CONNECTICUT

Published in the United States and Canada by
Greenwood Press, 88 Post Road West, Westport, CT 06881
an imprint of Greenwood Publishing Group, Inc.

English language edition, except the United States and Canada, published
by Flicks Books, England.

First published 1992

Library of Congress Cataloging in Publication Data

Shiri, Keith
    Directory of African film-makers and films / compiled and edited
by Keith Shiri
        p.   cm.
    Includes bibliographical references (p.   ) and indexes.
    ISBN 0-313-28756-2 (alk. paper)
    1. Motion picture producers and directors--Africa--Directories.
2. Motion pictures--Africa--Catalogs.   I. Title.
PN1993.5.A35S48 1992
016.79143'0233'09226--dc20   92-22105
                                                                  CIP

Library of Congress Catalog Card Number: 92-22105

ISBN: 0-313-28756-2

Contents

Acknowledgements

I owe thanks to many people who have helped me in various ways in compiling this book. Firstly and most importantly I must thank all the film-makers who provided information on their careers and filmography by questionnaire and correspondence. Of the 259 film-makers profiled, some 75% helped in this way.

I would also like to thank the following individuals and organisations:

Lars Åhlander at the Swedish Film Institute in Stockholm; Mohamed Amin at Camerapix in Kenya; Roy Armes; Martine Leroy at l'Association des Trois Mondes in Paris; Atriascop in Paris; Victor Bachy at OCIC in Brussels; Mariet Bakker; Françoise Balogun; Flavia Bianchi; Ferid Boughedir; the British Council; the British Film Institute Library; COE in Milan; Saad el-Din Wahba; FESPACO in Ouagadougou; E Gazzi at the Istituto Italiano di Cultura in London; the Ghana Film Industry Corporation in Accra; June Givanni; Amrik Heyer; Gastone Kabore; Mark Kaplan; Claude Le Gallou; Chantal Morel at the Institut Français in London; Lionel Ngakane; Nigeria High Commission, London; Françoise Pfaff; Elaine Proctor; Miriam Rosen; Dominique Wallon at the Centre National de la Cinématographie in Paris; Marlies Villwock at Filmförderungsanstalt in Berlin; the Visiting Arts of Great Britain; and my colleagues at the Africa Centre in London.

The publisher and I gratefully acknowledge the contribution of the following individuals who have provided specific help:

Ann Anderson at the South African Embassy in London checked the film titles in Afrikaans; Johan Blignaut of Showdata in Johannesburg provided useful information on some of the South African film-makers; translator Françoise Delas-Reisz helped with translating various film titles in French; Eugénio Lisboa, Cultural Counsellor at the Portuguese Embassy in London and translator Vera Hallam checked the film titles in Portuguese; Michael Mann and colleagues from the Department of Africa at the School of Oriental and African Studies at the University of London helped with identifying some of the film titles in African languages; Hashem el Nahas, President of the Egyptian Film Centre in Cairo and Professor Dr Hussein A A Sayed, Cultural Counsellor and Director at the Egyptian Education Bureau in London, both provided invaluable material and information relating to Egyptian film directors; Mr Nour-Eldin at the Egyptian-British Chamber of Commerce in London and Mohamed Said from the External Services Division at the School of Oriental and African Studies at the University of London checked the film titles in Arabic.

Finally, I must mention a special debt of gratitude to Tessa Carayan for her unfailing moral support and encouragement.

Keith Shiri
The Africa Centre
London
July 1992

Introduction

This book attempts to provide a single comprehensive reference guide to the most important and active directors who have been involved in feature, documentary and animation film production in 29 countries and states from the whole of the African continent over the last 60 years.

Entries are arranged alphabetically by director's surname, and a description of the country which he or she represents. Each entry consists of concise biographical information, including, where known, date and place of birth, details of educational and career achievements, followed by a list of films under **Filmography**.

Each filmography includes, wherever possible, all films made by the director. Films are listed by their date of production, followed by original language title(s), any alternative title(s) and English language title(s). The latter are either those which have been used by distributors outside the country of production or, more often, literal translations.

The second half of the book includes additional reference material. The *Film Title Index* includes some 3000 entries in all language versions listed in the directors' entries, together with those mentioned in the biographies. The *General Index* covers educational institutions, film organisations, titles of plays and books and personalities mentioned in the directors' entries. The *Country Index* is found at the front of the book. The index entries are arranged alphabetically; where a definite or indefinite article forms the first word of an entry and is not a numeral, it has been ignored in creating the alphabetical order. Accents and other diacritical marks also do not affect the alphabetical order. A *Selected Bibliography* details reference books and catalogues.

In each entry I have attempted to give as complete information as possible, but in a few cases some details could not be traced. The lack of full and reliable information on African film-makers, even sometimes of very basic facts, together with the various problems of extracting what information there is, have made the compilation of this book difficult. We can only hope that this deficiency will be remedied in the future by further research and easier access to documentation. I would welcome any comments, suggestions, corrections and additions, which may be sent to the publisher.

Explanatory Notes

In using this book readers are asked to bear in mind the following points:

- throughout the book every attempt has been made to include the original language spelling of film titles. Capital letters of French and Portuguese characters are not accented, except where they occur in a director's name.

- in some instances of film titles in the African language, the African languages are indicated in italic brackets, where known: for example (SEMBENE), Xala *[Wolof]*.

- where several foreign language titles are given, this usually indicates a co-production between two or more countries. The format is original language title / language title of co-producing country, followed by the English language title or translation.

- where the title of the film is the name of a person or place, this is often identical in English and therefore in these cases only the original title is listed.

- if another director is mentioned in a biography and that director is included in the book as a separate entry, his/her name is given in bold type. These references are given at the foot of each director's entry.

- for easier location in the indexes and cross-references, page numbers are followed by b (biography), or f (filmography): for example, 123f. Where two entries appear on one page, these are differentiated for the indexes as follows: 124/If and 124/IIf.

Abbreviations

The following abbreviations have been used in the directory:

aka	also known as [aka film title]
co-	'co-' preceding a function indicates collaboration
D	documentary film
dir(s)	director(s)
ep(s).	episode(s)
grad.	graduated

This book is dedicated to my mother

Country Index

African Film-Makers

ABDEL KHALEK, Ali   Egypt

5.9.1944 Cairo, Egypt. He studied at the Higher Cinema Institute in Cairo (grad. 1966).
Abdel Khalek worked as an assistant and also directed many short films before making his
feature début in 1972.

Filmography

1972	Oghnia 'ala al-Mamar / A Song on the Road
1976	A Home Without Tenderness
1980	Adhaab al-Hobb / The Torment of Love
	Al-Abalesa / The Devils
1981	Al-Hobb wahduh la yakfi / Not By Love Alone
	Musaffer bila tariq / Roadless Voyager
1982	Wada'at hobbi hunak / My Love Was Lost There
	Al-'ar / The Shame
1984	Al-Sada al-Mortashoon / The Bribed
	Banat iblis / Devil's Daughters / *aka* Daughters of Satan
1985	I 'dam mayyit / Execution of a Dead Man
	Al-Kayf / Hashish
1986	Shadir al-Samak / Fish Market
	Al-Hanakish
1987	Madafin mafrusha lil-igar / Furnished Tombs for Rent
	Al-Wahl / The Mud
	Bir al-Khayana / The Well of Treachery
	Arba'a fi muhimma rasmiyya / Four On an Official Mission
1988	Gary al-Wuhush / The Way of the Beasts
1989	Ilhaquna / Save Us
	Ightisab / Rape
1990	Al-Baida wal-hagar / The Egg and the Stone / *aka* The Charlatan / *aka* The Swindler

ABDEL SALAM, Shadi   Egypt

9.3.1930 Alexandria, Egypt; died 1986. He studied at the University of Oxford and at Cairo's Institute of Fine Arts, where he graduated with a degree in architecture (1955). Abdel Salam began working in the Egyptian film industry as an assistant on feature films (1957-59) and designed the costumes for *Al-Nasir Salah al-Din / Saladin* (**Chahine**, 1963). He was also assistant set designer on the Hollywood production *Cleopatra* (Joseph L Mankiewicz, 1963) and artistic advisor on the Polish feature *Faraon / Pharaoh* (Jerzy Kawalerowicz, 1965). From 1968 Abdel Salam worked with several visiting film-makers as assistant and artistic advisor. For many years he was director of Cairo's Experimental Film Centre. His début feature was internationally praised.

Filmography

1968	Al-Mumia / The Mummy / *aka* The Night of Counting the Years / *aka* The Night of the Counting of the Years
1970	Al-Fallah al fassih / The Eloquent Peasant
1972	Afaak / Horizons
1974	Gouyoush al chams / The Armies of the Sun
1982	Korsi Tout Ankh Amoun al Zahaby / The Gilded Chair of Tutankhamen
1984	Al-Ahramat wa ma kablaha / The Pyramids and the Preceding Period
1986	Aan Ramses el Sani / After Ramses II

ABDEL SAYED, Daoud   Egypt

1946 Cairo, Egypt. He graduated from the Higher Cinema Institute in Cairo and began to direct feature films through the National Centre for Documentary Films, also in Cairo. Abdel Sayed is a member of the New Egyptian Realist group of film-makers.

Filmography

1985	Al-Sa'alik / The Bums / *aka* The Vagabonds
1990	Al-Bahth 'an al-Sayyid Marzuq / Searching for Mr Marzuq / *aka* The Search for Sayed Marzuq

ABDELAZIZ, Tolbi   Algeria

1938 Constantine, north-eastern Algeria. He studied cinema at the Universität zu Köln in Germany and later worked for German television.

Filmography

1966	Algiers and Algeria
1968	Rendezvous in the Tropic of Cancer
1969	The Hunted Man
1970	The Cage
1971	The Key of the Enigma

ABIKANLOU, Pascal   Benin

1936 Sidi Alouane, Tunisia. He trained to be a photographer through a correspondence course and became a reporter and assistant cameraman. Abikanlou worked as a news cameraman before directing his first film (1967). His output has consisted mainly of documentaries; his only feature film is *Sous le signe du vaudou / Under the Sign of the Voodoo* (1974).

Filmography

1967	Ganvié mon village / Ganvié My Village
1968	Escale au Dahomey / Call at Dahomey
1969	Premières offrandes / First Offerings
	La fête de l'igname / Feast of Yams
1971	Opération SONADER / Operation SONADER
	De l'eau et de l'ombrage / Some Water and Shade
1974	Sous le signe du vaudou / Under the Sign of the Voodoo
1975	L'Afrique au rendez-vous de l'année sainte / Africa Gets Ready for the Holy Year

October 1950 Egypt. Son of the well-known Egyptian film-maker **Salah Abou Seif**. He studied at the American University in Cairo, specialising in psychology and drama (1968-72) and at the Higher Cinema Institute in Cairo (1971-76). He worked as an assistant director (1972-77) before making his own directorial début. Both his films are features.

Filmography

1986   Al-Tuffaha wal-gumguma / The Apple and the Skull
1988   Nahr al-Khawf / The River of Fear

See also: 5b.

10.5.1915 Boulaq, a district of Cairo. He was brought up by his mother and often spent his school time at the local cinema. He obtained a diploma in economics and commerce (1932) and then was a film critic for the magazines *Al-Sabah* and *Al-Aroussa*. He also worked for a short period in the cotton industry. Abou Seif began his film career as a trainee editor at Studio Misr (1934) and was director of the editing department there (1940-47). He also worked as an assistant, mainly to directors **Ahmed Badrakhan**, Niazi Mustapha, **Selim** and Yusuf Wahby. He was assistant director and assistant editor to Selim on his landmark film *Al-Azima / The Will* (1939). Abou Seif made many short films and documentaries (1940-42) and in 1946 he directed his first feature film, *Daiman fi qalbi / Always In My Heart*, an Egyptian version of Hollywood's *Waterloo Bridge* (Mervyn LeRoy, 1940). He is a founder member of the scriptwriting school in Cairo and has taught film at the Higher Cinema Institute there; he was also chairman of the Filmentag company (1963-65). *Lak yawm ya Zalim / Your Day Will Come* (1952) is a free adaptation of Zola's novel *Thérèse Raquin*. He remade Joseph Losey's *The Sleeping Tiger* (1954) in 1958 and *Letter from an Unknown Woman* (Max Ophuls, 1948) in 1962. Among his films are four adaptations of novels by the noted Egyptian writer Ihsan Abdel-Kuddous. Abou Seif's prolific output also includes many short documentaries: three on life in Sudan (1954); five on Egyptian folk music (1969); two on electricity in rural Egyptian villages (1976); and a series of four studies on folk art in Saudi Arabia (1984). His son **Mohamed Abou Seif** is also a film-maker.

Filmography

1940	Torok al-Naql fi Alaskandria / Methods of Transport in Alexandria
	Vawmoun fi mu'askar hindy / Journal of an Indian Camp
	Tarik al Mowassalat / The Big Road
1941	Simfuniyyat al Kahira / Symphony of Cairo
1942	Nemra Setta / Number 6
1946	Daiman fi qalbi / Always In My Heart
1947	Al-Muntaqim / The Avenger
1948	Mughamarat Antar wa Abla / The Adventures of Antar and Abla
1949	Shari' al-Bahlawan / Street of the Acrobat / *aka* Clown's Street
	Zal el sharr / Struggle Against Evil
	Nahwa Mogtamaa Gadidi / Towards a New Society
1950	Al-Saqr / The Falcon
1951	Al-Hubb bahdala / Love Is Scandalous
1952	Lak yawm ya Zalim / Your Day Will Come
1953	Al-Usta Hassan / Foreman Hassan
	Souk baladna / Our Home Market
	Raya wa Sakina / Raya and Sakina
1954	Al-Wahsh / The Monster
1955	Shabab imra'a / A Woman's Youth
	Al-Bitrul fi misr / Oil in Egypt
1956	Al-Futuwwa / The Bully

1957	Al-Wisada al-Khaliya / The Empty Pillow
	La anam / Night Without Sleep / *aka* No Sleep
1958	Mugrim fi agaza / A Thief on Vacation / *aka* A Thief's Holiday
	Al-Tariq al-Masdood / The Alley / *aka* Blocked Road
	Hadha huwwa al-hubb / The Real Love / *aka* That Is What Love Is
1959	Ana hurra / I Am Free
	Bayn al-Sama wal-ard / Between Heaven and Earth
1960	Law'at al-Hubb / The Anguish of Love / *aka* Agony of Love
	Bidaya wa nihaya / Death Among the Living / *aka* The Beginning and the End
	El Banat wal sayf / The Girls and the Summer
1961	La tutfi' al-Shams / Don't Put Out the Sun / *aka* The Sun Will Never Set
1962	Risala min imra'a majhula / Letter from an Unknown Woman
1963	La waqt lil-hubb / No Time for Love
1966	Al-Kahira thalathin / Cairo '30
1967	Al-Zaujat al-Thaniya / The Second Wife
1968	Al-Qadiya 68 / Case 68
1969	Thalath nisa'a / Three Women (one *ep.*)
1970	Shay'un min al-'adhab / A Certain Pain
	Fajr al-Islam / The Dawn of Islam
	Mala al Kassat / Filled the Glasses
	Belady Belady / My Country, My Country
	Aedoun / Returning
	Islamy ya Misr / Be Safe, Egypt
	Allah Akbar / God Is Great
1973	Hammam al-Malatili / The Baths of Malatili
1975	Al-Kaddab / The Liar
1976	Sana oula Hob / The First Year of Love (one *ep.*)
	Wa saqatat fi bahr min al-'asal / In an Ocean of Honey
1977	Al-Saqqa mat / The Water Carrier Is Dead
1978	Al-Mujrim / The Assassin / *aka* The Criminal
1980	Al-Qadisiya / The Qadisiya
1986	Al-Bidaya / The Beginning / *aka* The Empire of Satan
1990	Mewaten Masri / Egyptian Citizen / *aka* War on the Land of Egypt

See also: 4b.

ACHKAR, David   Guinea

1960 Guinea: Achkar studied cinema at the Ecole Supérieure d'Etudes Cinématographiques (ESEC) in Paris. He has written several unproduced film scripts and acted on the stage in various French companies.

Filmography

1983   Renaud-Barrault
1991   Allah Tantou / God's Will

ADEJUMO, Moses Olaiya   Nigeria

Nigeria. Also known as Baba Sala, his stage name. He is one of the best known Nigerian comedians, having appeared in many theatre and television plays.

Filmography

1983   Aare Agbaye *[Yoruba]* (co-dir Oyewole Olowomojuore)
1985   Mosebolatan *[Yoruba]*

ADJESO, Egbert Teye   Ghana

23.10.1931 Odumasi-Krobo in the eastern province of Ghana. Adjeso completed his secondary education in Achimota (1947-51). In 1952 he enrolled at the Gold Coast Film Unit (now the Ghana Film Industry Corporation) where he took a course in film production. Adjeso then went to London where he received further training at Pinewood Studios (1960). In 1964 he became a member of the British Kinematograph, Sound and Television Society. Adjeso was elected president of the Film Guild of Ghana (1983). His début film is a musical comedy.

Filmography

1970   I Told You So

ADU, Jabu   Nigeria

Lagos, Nigeria. As a child he spent most of his spare time in movie theatres and soon Adu wanted to be an actor. His parents took no notice of his ambition and sent him to London to study banking. He took evening courses in drama and on his return to Nigeria became involved in amateur theatre and radio. He played a part in a radio series and also wrote one episode; he also began writing and acting for television. Having achieved considerable popularity as an actor and scriptwriter for both radio and television, Adu started to work in film, firstly as a co-producer and actor in *Countdown At Kusini* (1976), an American-Nigerian co-production directed by Ossie Davis, and later that year as a director.

Filmography

1976   Bisi, Daughter of the River

AKANDO, Séverin   Benin

1952 Benin. He studied literature at the Université Nationale du Bénin in Cotonou. After graduation he was awarded a scholarship to study cinematography in Moscow. On his return to Benin, Akando began to work for national television. His début film is a documentary on the life of Patrice Lumumba (1926-61), the first prime minister of Zaïre.

Filmography

1984   Histoire d'une vie / Story of a Life
        Abomey

AKIN, Mohamed Lamine   Guinea

1927 Treichville, a suburb of Abidjan, Ivory Coast. He studied cinema at the Institut des Hautes Etudes Cinématographiques (IDHEC) in Paris.

Filmography

1966   Le sergent Bakary Woolen / Sergeant Bakary Woolen
        Mary Narken
        Dans la vie des peuples il y a des instants / In the Life of Peoples There
           Are Moments

See also: 53/IIb.

AKOMFRAH, John   Ghana

1957 Ghana. He completed his studies in London. In 1983 Akomfrah founded the Black Audio Film Collective (BAFC), a production collective for black directors and producers. He has worked as a freelance journalist for several years and has also organised courses on the cinema for the British Film Institute and the University of London. He made his début as a film director in 1986 with *Handsworth Songs*, a medium-length film which confronts the problems of racism in Britain.

Filmography

1986	Handsworth Songs
1988	Testament

AKOUISSONE, Joseph   Central African Republic

3.3.1943 Bangassou, Central African Republic. He received his early education in Bangassou and Bangui. Akouissone spent most of his spare time at movie theatres and became interested in making films. He went to Paris where he studied cinematography at the Université de Paris VIII. Returning home, he worked with the local television station, producing several programmes. In 1974 he directed his first film *Josepha*; all his films have been documentaries.

Filmography

1974	Josepha
1977	Festival de Royan / Royan Festival
1980	Dieux noirs du stade / Black Gods of the Stadium
1981	Zo-Kwe-Zo / Un homme est un homme / A Man Is a Man
1986	Burkina cinéma / Cinema in Burkina Faso
1987	FESPACO Images 87
1989	Africa cinéma / African Cinema

AL-BAKRI, Asma   Egypt

Cairo, Egypt. She studied literature at Alexandria University and history at Cairo University. Al-Bakri entered the film industry as an assistant director and director of production on more than thirty films. Between 1975 and 1990 she worked as a journalist before making her first film.

Filmography

1991   Mendiants et orgueilleux / The Beggars and the Proud

AL-DIK, Beshir   Egypt

27.7.1944 Damietta, Lower Egypt. He completed his secondary schooling in Damietta and then studied commerce at Cairo University (grad. 1966). Al-Dik began working in the cinema as a scriptwriter (1978-87) for directors Tayssir Aboud, Ashraf Fahmy, Atef Salem, **Yashfin** and notably on five films for **Khan**, including *Al-Th'ar / Vengeance* (1980), *Tair 'alal-tariq / Bird on the Road* (1981) and *Al-Harrif / Streetplayer* (1983). He also wrote short stories which were published in Egyptian and Iraqi newspapers and magazines (early 1970s). Al-Dik made his directorial début in 1985.

Filmography

1985   Al-Tufan / The Flood / *aka* The Deluge / *aka* The Wreck
1986   Sikket safar / The Journey's Road / *aka* Route of Departure

AL-MAANOUNI, Ahmed   Morocco

1944 Casablanca, Morocco. He studied at the Institut National des Arts du Spectacle et Techniques de Diffusion (INSAS) in Brussels, Belgium and made his début as a director in 1978.

Filmography

1975	Tabouka Festival
1976	Immigrant's Childhood
1978	Al-Ayyam, al-Ayyam / Oh These Days / *aka* Oh the Days, Oh the Days
1980	Ahwal / Trances

AL-MIHI, Raafat   Egypt

25.9.1940 Cairo, Egypt. Al-Mihi studied English literature at Cairo University (grad. 1960). He then studied scriptwriting (1962-64) and worked as a scriptwriter for television and the cinema (1965-75). Al-Mihi has also written extensively for Egyptian newspapers.

Filmography

1980	'Uyun la tanam / Unsleeping Eyes / *aka* Eyrie
1984	Al-Avocato / The Lawyer
1986	Lil-hubb qissa akhira / A Last Love Story / *aka* Broken Images
1987	Al-Sada al-Rijal / The Gentlemen
1988	Samak, laban, tamar hindi / Hurley-Burley
1990	Sayyidati, annisati / Demoiselles / Ladies and Young Ladies

See also: 13b.

5.2.1919 Egypt. After completing his secondary education he worked as an assistant in the editing department at Studio Misr under the direction of Niazi Mustapha. He became one of the best known Egyptian film editors before making his first film as a director in 1952. His feature film output since then has been prolific. In 1975 he started a production company with scriptwriter and director **Al-Mihi**. In 1980 Al-Sheikh became head of the Cinema Committee at the Egyptian Ministry of Culture in Cairo.

Filmography

1952	Al-Manzel Rakam 13 / House No. 13
1953	Al-Mo'amra / The Plot
1954	Haya Aw Mout / Life and Death
1955	Hob wa Demou'e / Love and Tears
1956	Al-Gharib / The Stranger
	Hob wa E'edam / Love and Execution
1957	Ard Al-Salam / Peace Land / *aka* Land of Peace
	Ard Al-Ahlam / Dream Land
	Toggar Al-Mout / Death Merchants
1958	Al-Malak Al-Saghir / The Small Angel
	Sayedat Al-Kasr / Lady of the Palace
1959	Men Agl Emra'a / For a Woman
	Kalb Yahtarek / Burning Heart
1960	Malak wa Shaytan / Angel and Devil
	Hobi Al-Wahid / My Single Love
1961	Lan A'taref / I Shall Not Confess
1962	Al-Less Wel Kelab / The Thief and the Dogs
1963	Al-Shaytan Al-Saghir / The Young Devil
	Al-Leila Al-Akhira / The Last Night
1965	El Kha'ena / The Unfaithful
1966	Thalas Lossos / Three Thieves
1967	Al-Mokharreboun / The Destroyers
1968	Al-Ragol Alazi Fakad Zelo / The Man Who Lost His Shadow
1969	Miramare
	Beer Al-Herman / Well of Deprivation
1970	Ghoroub wa Shorouk / Sunset and Sunrise
1971	Shay'oun Fi Sadri / Profound Secret
1974	Al-Hareb / The Fugitive
1975	Ala Man Natlok Al-Rassass / At Whom We Must Shoot
1976	Sana Oula Hob / The First Year of Love (one *ep.*)
1978	Wa Thalesshom Al-Shaytan / Their Third Was the Devil
	El Seyoud Eln Eya Maweya / Ascent to the Abyss
1982	Al-Tawoos / The Peacock
1986	Kaher Al-Zaman / The Conqueror of Time

26.12.1947 Cairo, Egypt. In 1966 Al-Tayyeb began studying at the Higher Cinema Institute in Cairo (grad. 1970). He then completed his military service and spent five years in the army. He made two short films (1972-76) and worked as assistant to **Abdel Salam** on *Gouyoush al chams / The Armies of the Sun* (1974) and to **Chahine** on his important film *Iskandariya... leeh? / Alexandria... Why?* (1978). His directorial début in the cinema (1982) is a modern adaptation of Shakespeare's *Othello*.

Filmography

1982	Al-Ghira al-Katila / Murderous Jealousy
1983	Sawwaq al-Autobis / The Bus Driver
1984	Al-Takhshiba / The Clink / *aka* The Cell
1985	Al-Zammar / The Piper
1986	Malaff fil-adaab / On File for Morals
	Al-Bare'a / The Innocent
	Al-Hubb fawq al-Haram / Love Above the Pyramid
1987	Al-Badrum / The Basement
1988	Abna' wa qatala / Sons and Killers
	Al-Donya 'ala ganah yamama / The World on a Wing of a Dove
1989	Katibat al-I'dam / Firing Squad
	Qalb al-Layl / Heart of the Night
1990	Al-Horoub / The Escape
1991	Nagi Al-Ali

1942 Djougou, north-western Benin. He was born into a very large Yoruba and Muslim family. When Alassane was eleven years old the family moved to Niger. After finishing primary school he worked as a mechanic's apprentice and as a truck driver. He spent most of his spare time watching French films at his local movie theatre. He gave up truck driving to work as a clerk at the Institut Fondamental d'Afrique Noire (IFAN). He started hand-painting films using colour dyes; his experiments were noticed by the French ethnologist and film-maker Jean Rouch, who helped Alassane acquire basic training in film-making. Shortly afterwards he studied ethnographic film-making in Paris (1962) and a year later took a nine-month training course in film-making and animation with Norman McLaren at the National Film Board of Canada in Montreal. In 1965 he made a short animation film *La mort de Gandji / Gandji's Death*, regarded as the first produced in Africa, which won the prize for best short film at the Dakar Film Festival; he has since made several other animation films. Alassane has acted in several films and served as a jury member at various international film festivals. With **Ganda** he is considered a pioneer of Niger cinema.

Filmography

1962	Le piroguier / The Canoe Paddler
	La pileuse de mil / Woman Pounding Millet
	Aouré *[Hausa]* / Mariage / Marriage
1964	La bague du roi Koda / King Koda's Ring
1965	La mort de Gandji / Gandji's Death
1966	L'arachide de Sanchira / The Sanchira Peanut
	Le retour d'un aventurier / An Adventurer's Return
	Bon voyage, Sim
1971	Deela ou el Barka le conteur / Deela or el Barka the Story-Teller
	Jamya
1972	Femme, villa, voiture, argent / Wife, Villa, Car, Money / *aka* FVVA
	Sakhi
1973	Toula ou le génie des eaux / Toula or The Water Spirit (co-dir Anna Söhring)
1975	Samba le grand / Samba the Great
	Souabane
1979	Festival à Dosso / Festival at Dosso
1982	Kankamba ou le semeur de discorde / *aka* L'indiscret inconscient / Kankamba or the Spreader of Discord
1984	Kokoa

See also: 67/IIb.

6.10.1944 Algiers, Algeria. Allouache studied cinema at the Institut National du Cinéma in Algiers.

Filmography

1967	El Bouhai
1968	Les plages / The Beaches
1973	Nous et la révolution agraire / The Agrarian Revolution and Us
1975	Vent du sud / South Wind
1976	Omar Gatlato
1978	Mughamarat batal / Les aventures d'un héros / The Adventures of a Hero
1982	Rajul wa Nawafidh / L'homme qui regardait les fenêtres / The Man Who Watched Windows / *aka* Man and Windows
1986	Un amour à Paris / A Paris Love / *aka* A Romance in Paris

AMIN, Mohamed   Kenya

29.8.1943 Nairobi, Kenya. He was educated at secondary school in Dar es Salaam, Tanzania. In his teens he worked as a photojournalist (1958-61) and then started his own film production company, Camerapix (1963). From 1963 to the present Amin has worked on films for television as a cameraman, producer and/or director. Among his films as a producer are *A Fragile Future* (1985), *Give Me Shelter* (1987), *Battle on the Roof of the World* (1989) and *Defenders of Pakistan* (1991); his documentaries and news journalism have won many international awards. Amin is also a prolific author and publisher of over forty books and publications on history, culture, landscape, wildlife and the environment in such countries as Kenya, Maldives, Nepal, Pakistan and Zimbabwe (from 1969). He has been chairman of the Foreign Correspondents Association of East Africa (1978-1983; 1991 to present) and since 1987 chairman of Samburu Aid in Africa (SAIDIA). He has also been head of the African bureau of Visnews since 1966. Amin received the Member of the Order of the British Empire (MBE) in 1991 for services to photography and journalism in Africa.

Filmography

    1979   Hunters of the Jade Sea
    1985   African Calvary
    1986   Tomorrow's Famine
    1988   Organization of African Unity

AMPAW, King   Ghana

1940 Ghana. After studying film-making at various schools in Munich, Potsdam-Babelsberg and Vienna, Ampaw worked for German television. He directed his début feature film in West Germany. Ampaw returned to Ghana (1986) and started to work with the Ghana Broadcasting Corporation.

Filmography

1972	They Call It Love
1983	Kukurantumi: The Road to Accra
1986	Juju (co-dir Ingrid Metner)

ANSAH, Kwaw Paintsil   Ghana

7.7.1941 Agona Swedru, Ghana. He was influenced by his father who was a photographer. Ansah left school at an early age and became a draftsman. He became skilled in textiles whilst working at the United Africa Company and Unilever in Ghana. Ansah left Ghana for England to join his cousin, film-maker **Aato Yarney,** who encouraged his interest in the cinema. He studied theatre design at the Polytechnic of Central London as well as taking drama courses at the American Musical and Dramatic Academy. He was then awarded a grant to study film production at RKO Studios in California, United States. Whilst there, Ansah wrote two plays which were produced: *The Adoption* and *A Mother's Tears*. He returned to Ghana where he became production assistant at the Ghana Film Industry Corporation. After a few years he left to work for Unilever's Lintas Advertising and Target Advertising Services and produced some short films. It was not until 1977 that Ansah decided to become an independent film-maker: together with some friends he formed Film Africa Limited, an Accra-based film production unit.

Filmography

1980	Love Brewed in the African Pot
1987	Heritage... Africa

See also: 153/Ib.

ARAFA, Sharif   Egypt

25.12.1960 Cairo, Egypt. He studied at the Higher Cinema Institute in Cairo (grad. 1983) where he made several short films. He also worked as an assistant (1976-85). All his films to date have been documentaries.

Filmography

1987	Al-Aqzam qadimun / The Dwarfs Are Coming
1988	Al-Daraja al-Thalitha / The Third Class
1990	Sama' huss / Listen and Shut Up / *aka* Silence!
1991	Ya Mahalabeya Ya

ASCOFARE, Abdoulaye   Mali

1949 Bamako, Mali. Ascofare studied cinema at VGIK in Moscow. His first film is a short documentary on the South African writer Alex Lagroi. His two short films *M'sieur Fané / Mr Fané* and *L'hôte / The Host*, made during his studies in Moscow, were presented at the Festival Panafricain du Cinéma de Ouagadougou (FESPACO) in 1983.

Filmography

1982	Welcome
1983	M'sieur Fané / Mr Fané
	L'hôte / The Host

AUGE, Simon   Gabon

15.12.1944 Port Gentil, Gabon. He completed his primary and secondary education in Port Gentil and Libreville. He started work as a radio journalist. Auge then went to France where he studied both cinematography and television production. In 1985 he became the director of the National Film Institute of Gabon. He made his first film *Où vas-tu, Koumba?* / *Where Are You Going, Koumba?* in 1971.

Filmography

1971	Où vas-tu, Koumba? / Where Are You Going, Koumba? (co-dir Alain Ferrari)
1974	Il était une fois Libreville / Once Upon a Time Libreville
1976	Mbigou, poésie du Gabon / Mbigou, Poetry from Gabon
1982	La femme blanche / The White Woman

See also: 59/lb.

AW, Cheikh Tidiane   Senegal

1935 Kébèmer, Senegal. He completed his early primary and secondary education in Kébèmer and studied cinema in West Germany and at OCORA/Radio France in Paris. Returning to Senegal, Aw worked for Senegalese television where he was the producer of several programmes. In 1969 he made his first film, the documentary *N'Doep* / *Réalités* / *Realities*. He has also made three feature films (1971-81).

Filmography

1969	N'Doep / Réalités / Realities
1971	Serigné Assagne / Pour ceux qui savent / For Those Who Know / *aka* Those Who Know
1974	Le bracelet de bronze / The Bronze Bracelet
1981	Le certificat / The Certificate
1983	Soins de santé primaires / Primary Health Care

AZIZ, Mohamed Nadir   Algeria

20.10.1941 Miliana, Algeria. He studied cinema at the Institut National du Cinéma in Algiers.

Filmography

1973	Festival panafricain de la jeunesse / Panafrican Youth Festival
	L'homme de l'atlas / The Atlas Man
1978	L'olivier de Boulhilet / The Olive-Tree of Boulhilet
1984	Hommage à l'Emir Abdelakader / Homage to Emir Abdelakader

BA, Cheikh Ngaïdo   Senegal

10.6.1949 Piré, western Senegal. He worked initially as a television director and producer before making three short uncompleted films (1973-76). He made his feature début in 1978.

Filmography

1973	La brosse / The Brush
1974	Arrêté car / Stopped Because
1976	Tablo feraay
1978	Rewo daande mayo [Peul] / De l'autre côté du fleuve / From the Other Side of the River
1983	Xew-Xew [Wolof] / La fête commence / Let the Party Begin
1985	Opération Niebe / Operation Niebe

BA KOBHIO, Bassek   Cameroon

1957 Cameroon. Both his parents were teachers. Whilst still at school Ba Kobhio wanted to become a writer. During his fourth year at secondary school he won a literature competition; the prize was a book on **Sembene**, the famous Senegalese writer, historian and film-maker. This triggered two dreams - to become a writer and to become a film-maker. In 1976 he enrolled at the Université de Yaoundé where he graduated in sociology and philosophy (grad. 1978). He then worked as a literary critic for Cameroon Radio and also taught at a local grammar school (1978-85). After leaving teaching he worked for the Ministry of Information as an assistant director of films. In 1988 he worked as an assistant director with French film-maker Claire Denis on her film *Chocolat* and made his own début as a director that year.

Filmography

1988   FESTAC 88
1991   Sango Malo / Le maître du canton / *aka* Chronique d'une saison paysanne
        / The Master of the District

BABAÏ, Brahim   Tunisia

1936 Tunisia. He studied at the Institut des Hautes Etudes Cinématographiques (IDHEC) in Paris and then worked as a director of photography for Tunisian television. He has directed and produced many short and full-length films. *Wa ghadan / Et demain / And Tomorrow* (1971), which he directed and co-scripted, won awards at the International Film Festival of Carthage in Tunis, the Karlovy Vary Film Festival in Czechoslovakia, as well as the Jury Prize and the International Critics Prize at Cannes. It was also chosen at the Forum of Young Cinema in Berlin.

Filmography

1971   Wa ghadan / Et demain / And Tomorrow
        Victoire d'un peuple / Victory of a People
1990   La nuit de la décennie / The Night of the Decade

BADIE, Mustapha   Algeria

1928 Algiers, Algeria. Badie studied cinema at the Institut National du Cinéma in Algiers. After graduation he worked for national television where he made a number of short documentaries.

Filmography

1963   Nos mères / Our Mothers
1965   La nuit a peur du soleil / The Night Is Afraid of the Sun
1969   Essaher
1974   L'evasion de Hassan Terro / Hassan Terro's Escape
1977   Suicide

See also: 35/IIb.

18.10.1909 Cairo, Egypt; died 23.4.1969. He worked as assistant to Fritz Kramp on *Widad* (1936) and made his directorial début a year later. He has also made a few short films, including two in 1963. His son **Ali Badrakhan** is also a film-maker.

Filmography

1937	Nashid al-Amal / The Song of Hope
1938	Shuya min al-Shuya / Something of Nothing
1940	Dananir
	Intisar ash-shabab / Victory of Youth
1941	Assefa alal Rif / Thunderstorm Over the Countryside
1942	Ala Masrah el Haya / The Theatre of Life
	Aida
1944	Al-Abriyaa / The Innocents
	Man al Gani / Who Is the Criminal?
1945	Kobla fi Lobnan / A Kiss in the Lebanon
	Al-Gil el Gadid / The New Generation
	Taxi wa Hantour / Taxi and Backlash
	Ma Kadarche / I Cannot
1946	Awdat al Kafela / Return of the Group
	Al-Nafkha el Kadaba / Foolish Pride
1947	Al-Kahira - Baghdad / Cairo - Baghdad
	Kabelni ya Abi / Embrace Me, Daddy
1948	Fatma
1949	Ahebak Enta / I Love You
	Ana we Enta / Me and You
1950	Akher Kedba / Last Lie
1951	Leilat Gharam / One Night of Love
1952	Al-Iman / Faith
1953	Ayza Atgawez / I Want To Get Married
	Mustapha Kamel
	Lahn Hobi / Symphony of My Love
1954	Alashan Oyounak / For Your Eyes
	Wa'ed / Promise
1955	Ahd al-Hawa / Promise of Love
	Allah ma'na / God Is With Us
1956	Ezay Ansak / How To Forget You
1958	Ghariba / Foreigner
1963	Ila Arafat Allah
	Port-Said
1966	Sayed Darwish
1967	Al-Nisf al-Akhar / The Other Party
	Afrah / Marriages
	Gawab / Letter
1969	Nadia

See also: 5b, 25/lb.

BADRAKHAN, Ali   Egypt

1946 Cairo, Egypt. Son of the notable Egyptian film-maker **Ahmed Badrakhan** with whom he worked as an assistant. He studied at the Higher Cinema Institute in Cairo and worked with **Chahine** on his film *Al-Ikhtiyar / The Choice* (1970).

Filmography

1971	Al-Hubb aladhi kan / The Love That Was
1975	Al-Karnak
1981	Ahl al-Qimma / High Society
1986	Al-Ju' / Hunger

BAKABA, Sijiri   Ivory Coast

Also known as Sidiki Bakaba. 1949 Abengourou, south-eastern Ivory Coast. He has worked in the theatre and was the leading actor in many productions in the Ivory Coast (1963-82). Bakaba has also appeared in many television films and serials and acted in more than a dozen films, including *Le médecin de Gafiré / Gafiré's Doctor* (**Mustapha Diop**, 1982), *Visages de femmes / Faces of Women* (**Ecaré**, 1985), *Camp de Thiaroye / Camp Thiaroye* (**Sembene** and **Sow**, 1988) and his own *Les guérisseurs / Aduefue, Lords of the Street* (1988).

Filmography

1984	L'aventure ambiguë / The Ambiguous Adventure
1988	Les guérisseurs / Aduefue, Lords of the Street / *aka* The Healers

BAKABE, Mahamane   Niger

1947 Gazaoua, Niger. After completing his studies he became a primary school teacher.
He studied cinematography at the Institut National de l'Audiovisuel (INA) at Bry-sur-Marne
in Paris and on his return worked for national television. He produced numerous television
documentaries before directing his first feature film *Le barrage de Kandji / The Dam of
Kandji* in 1982.

Filmography

1976	La marmite / The Cooking Pot
1977	L'habitat / Habitat
	Pèlerinage à La Mecque / Pilgrimage to Mecca
1978	Un homme et sa musique / A Man and His Music
1980	L'avenir d'Ali et les autres / The Future of Ali and the Others
1981	Si les cavaliers... / If the Horsemen...
1982	Le barrage de Kandji / The Dam of Kandji
1983	Le grand combat pour l'autosuffisance alimentaire / The Great Battle for Alimentary Self-Sufficiency

BAKUPA-KANYINDA, Balufu   Zaïre

30.10.1957 Kinshasa, Zaïre. On completing his secondary schooling he went to Brussels
where he studied sociology, history and philosophy.

Filmography

1991	Thomas Sankara
	Dix mille ans de cinéma / Ten Thousand Years of Cinema

1956 Bauchi, northern Nigeria. Balewa studied film at the National Film and Television School in Beaconsfield, England. He has worked with the Performing Arts Company in Zaria in northern Nigeria and for the Nigerian Television Authority as a drama producer. He also briefly taught drama at the Ahmadu Bello University in Zaria.

Filmography

1990   Kasarmu Ce

1945 Aba, southern Nigeria. His father was a lawyer of Yoruba origin. Balogun attended secondary schooling in Lagos and then took courses in French at the Université Cheikh Anta Diop de Dakar in Senegal (1962). In 1963 Balogun went to Paris, enrolling at the Institut des Hautes Etudes Cinématographiques (IDHEC), where he studied film-making, and at the Université de Nanterre where he produced a doctoral dissertation on the documentary film. He returned to Nigeria (1967) and worked as a scriptwriter for the Federal Film Unit, before becoming press attaché at the Nigerian Embassy in Paris. Again returning to Nigeria, he became a research fellow in cinema at the University of Ife (1971). In 1972 Balogun completed his first feature film *Alpha*. In the following year he founded a production company, Afrocult Foundation. Balogun is one of Nigeria's best known and most prolific film-makers, making both documentaries and feature films which often incorporate Yoruba theatrical tradition. He is also a playwright and author of a number of short stories. Balogun is a founding member of the West African Film Corporation, the regional consortium for the production and distribution of West African films. He has made several films in the Yoruba language.

Filmography

1969	One Nigeria
1971	Les ponts de Paris / The Bridges of Paris
	Fire in the Afternoon
1972	Thundergod
	Alpha
	Nupe Mascarade
1973	Owuama, a New Year Festival
	Eastern Nigeria Revisited
1974	Vivre / To Live
1975	Nigersteel
	Amadi *[Ibo]*
1976	Ajani-Ogun *[Yoruba]*
	Musik-Man / Music Man
1977	Ija Ominira *[Yoruba]* / Fight for Freedom
1978	A deusa negra / Black Goddess
1979	Aîye *[Yoruba]*
1981	Cry Freedom
1982	Orun Mooru *[Yoruba]*
	Money Power (in 2 parts)

See also: 107/IIb.

BANDE, Jean-Claude   Burkina Faso

1957 Ouagadougou, Burkina Faso. He studied film at the Ecole Supérieure d'Etudes Cinématographiques (ESEC) in Paris. He has been working with the National Film Institute since 1978.

Filmography

1987   Conférence nationale des C.D.R. / National Conference of the CDR
1989   Sibidou

BASSORI, Timité   Ivory Coast

30.12.1933 Aboisso near Abidjan, Ivory Coast. He is of Mandingo origin and Muslim extraction. After leaving school at the age of sixteen, he studied business at the Collège Technique d'Abidjan (grad. 1952). He started working as a clerk and spent most of his spare time watching American and French films. By 1956 he had saved sufficient money to go to France where he registered at the Cours Simon (Institut d'Art Dramatique) and later at the Centre d'Art Dramatique de la rue Blanche where he studied classical French theatre. After a period performing plays by writers such as Puškin at cultural centres in Paris, Bassori enrolled at the Institut des Hautes Etudes Cinématographiques (IDHEC) in Paris to study film-making (1958-61). He worked for a short period for French television and then returned to the Ivory Coast (1962) to work for the Société Ivoirienne de Cinéma (SIC). He worked closely with Radiodiffusion Télévision Ivoirienne (RTI) in Abidjan, where he produced several documentaries. In 1964 Bassori directed his first short feature film *Sur la dune de la solitude / On the Dune of Solitude*.

Filmography

1963   Les forestiers / The Foresters
          L'Abidjan-Niger / Abidjan-Niger
          Amédée Pierre
1964   Sur la dune de la solitude / On the Dune of Solitude
1966   Le sixième sillon / The Sixth Furrow
1967   Feux de brousse / Bush Fires
1968   La femme au couteau / The Woman With a Knife
1971   Abidjan, perle des lagunes / Abidjan, the Lagoon Pearl
          Bondoukou, an 11 / Bondoukou, Year 11
1972   Odienné, an 12 / Odienné, Year 12
          Kossou 1
1974   Kossou 2
          Les compagnons d'Akati / The Akati Fellows

BATHILY, Moussa Yoro   Senegal

1946 near Bakel, eastern Senegal. He is of Muslim extraction. After secondary school Bathily enrolled at the Université Cheikh Anta Diop de Dakar (1968) where he read history. He taught history for three years at the Lycée Abdoulaye Sadji in Rufisque. After leaving teaching, Bathily returned to Dakar where he joined the Dakar ciné-club and met Senegalese film-makers **Diop-Mambéty** and **Mahama Johnson Traoré**. He became deeply interested in cinema and started to write film scripts. Later he met **Sembene** who employed him as his trainee assistant during the filming of *Xala* (1974) and *Ceddo* (1976). In 1974 he made his first short films. Bathily is also a noted writer of film reviews, and articles and essays on cinema. He has founded his own production company, EMEBE Diffusion Films.

Filmography

1974	Fidak
	Centre international de Dakar / Dakar International Centre
1975	N'Dakarou *[Wolof]* / Dakar Morning Impressions
1976	Des personnages encombrants / Cumbersome People / *aka* Awkward People
1978	Tiyabu Biru *[Soninke]* / La circoncision / The Circumcision
1981	Le certificat d'indigence / Certificate of Nationality
	Siggi ou la poliomyélite / Siggi or Polyomyelitis
1983	Des sites et des monuments au Sénégal / Senegalese Sites and Monuments
1989	Petits blancs au manioc et à la sauce gombo / Poor Whites With Cassave and Gombo Sauce
1990	Biliyaanne

BEHI, Ridha   Tunisia

7.8.1947 Kairouan, Tunisia. He studied literature and social sciences at university in Tunis where he graduated with a masters degree in socio-ethnography. He later completed a PhD thesis on the subject "Cinema and Society in Tunisia during the Sixties". He made his first full-length film *Shams al-Diba / Sun of Hyenas* in 1975.

Filmography

1969	The Woman Statue
1972	Forbidden Thresholds
1975	Shams al-Diba / Sun of Hyenas / *aka* Hyena's Sun
1984	Al-Malaika / The Angels
1986	La mémoire écarlate / Scarlet Memory

BEKOLO, Jean-Pierre   Cameroon

8.6.1966 Yaoundé, Cameroon. After completing his secondary education he trained as a television editor at the Institut National de l'Audiovisuel (INA) at Bry-sur-Marne in Paris. He then worked as an editor for Cameroon radio and television. He also directed and produced several documentaries and music videos for musicians such as Manu Dibango.

Filmography

1992   Quarter Mozart

BELHIBA, Fitouri   Tunisia

January 1950 Zarzis, south-eastern Tunisia. He was a teacher for a period before becoming a stage actor. Belhiba has worked on several television documentaries.

Filmography

1988   Ragaya / Hopes

BELOUFA, Farouk   Algeria

20.4.1947 Algeria. He studied cinema at the Institut National du Cinéma in Algiers and at the Institut des Hautes Etudes Cinématographiques (IDHEC) in Paris. He made two diploma films: *Situation de Transition / Transitory Situation* and *Travesties and Breakages*.

Filmography

1970   L'aviation algérienne / Algerian Aviation
1971   Les imprimeries de l'ANP / The Printing Works of the ANP
1973   Guerre de libération / War of Liberation
1976   Le retour de l'enfant prodigue / The Return of the Prodigal Child
1979   Nahla

BEN, Aïcha Sadok   Tunisia

13.1.1936 Sidi Alouane, Tunisia. He received his primary and secondary education in Sfax and then enrolled at university in Tunis where he studied social sciences and humanities. Ben worked briefly as an assistant director for French radio and television and simultaneously studied cinematography at the Institut des Hautes Etudes Cinématographiques (IDHEC) in Paris; he also studied in Rome. On his return to Tunisia, he worked for Tunisian radio and television as a producer of several films.

Filmography

1966	Une lettre / A Letter
1967	Quand l'esprit s'amuse / Mind Games
1968	Mokhtar
1969	Combat de chameaux / Camel Fight
1978	Le mannequin / The Model

See also: 39/Ib.

BEN, Halima Hamouda   Tunisia

10.2.1935 Moknine, eastern Tunisia. After secondary school he enrolled at the Institut des Hautes Etudes Cinématographiques (IDHEC) in Paris to study cinematography and specialised in editing. He subsequently worked as an editor for Tunisian television before making his first short film *De la terre et des hommes / Earth and People* in 1962.

Filmography

1962	De la terre et des hommes / Earth and People
1963	Folklore à Monastir / Folklore in Monastir

BEN AMMAR, Abdellatif   Tunisia

25.4.1943 Tunis, Tunisia. He received his primary and secondary education in Tunis. He studied mathematics before registering at the Institut des Hautes Etudes Cinématographiques (IDHEC) in Paris to study cinematography (grad. 1964). In 1968 he made his first film *L'espérance / Hope*. Ben Ammar has worked as a cameraman for Canadian television and was director of production on *Jesus of Nazareth* (Franco Zeffirelli, 1978). He has formed his own production company, Latif Films.

Filmography

1968	L'espérance / Hope
1969	Une simple histoire / A Simple Story
1974	Sejnane
	Kairouan
1980	Aziza...

BEN BARKA, Souheil   Morocco

1942 Timbuktu, Mali. He made a series of television documentaries before directing his first full-length film in 1974.

Filmography

1969	Aqua
1971	Malika
1972	Alf yad wa yad / Mille et une mains / A Thousand and One Hands
1974	La guerre du pétrole n'aura pas lieu / The Petroleum War Will Not Take Place

BEN MAHMOUD, Mahmoud   Tunisia

1949 Tunis, Tunisia. He is a graduate of the Institut National des Arts du Spectacle et Techniques de Diffusion (INSAS), the film school in Brussels. He has also studied archaeology and journalism and written film scripts.

Filmography

1982   'Ubur / Crossings
1991   Chich Khan

BENDEDDOUCHE, Ghaouti   Algeria

25.3.1936 Tlemcen, north-western Algeria. He studied cinema at the Institut des Hautes Etudes Cinématographiques (IDHEC) in Paris. He worked as an assistant director on the Algerian film *La nuit a peur du soleil / The Night Is Afraid of the Sun* (**Badie**, 1965). Between 1964 and 1972 Bendeddouche made many documentaries, mainly for Algerian television. In 1976 he made his feature film début with *Echebka*.

Filmography

1964   Couleurs d'Algérie / Colours of Algeria
1967   Al-Jaza'ir
        Carrefour d'échanges / Crossroads of Exchange
        Le militant / The Militant
        Deglet Nour
        Aurès, terre de courage / Aurès, Land of Courage
1968   La mer / The Sea
        Les métiers à tisser / Weaving Looms
        La tannerie / The Tannery
        Puzzle et mozaïque / Puzzle and Mosaic
1969   Archie Sherp
        Magie de la main / Sleight of Hand
        La poterie / The Pottery
1970   La course du soleil / The Course of the Sun
1972   Assihar Na Ahaggar
        Festival panafricain de la jeunesse / Panafrican Youth Festival
1976   Echebka
1979   Morte la longue nuit / The Long Night Is Dead
1983   Moisson d'acier / Steel Harvest

BESHARA, Khairy   Egypt

30.6.1947 Tanta, Lower Egypt. He studied cinema at the Egyptian Higher Institute (grad. 1967). He worked as an assistant director on two feature films, *I Am the Doctor* (Abbas Kamel) and *Yawmiyyat na'ib fil-aryaf / Diary of the Village Investigator* (**Tewfik Saleh**, 1968) before studying in Poland on a one-year fellowship (1968-69). On his return to Egypt, Bashara continued to work as an assistant director and also acted and wrote scripts. He also appears in cameo roles in films by colleagues and is one of the New Egyptian Realist directors.

Filmography

1982	Al-Aqdar al-Damiya / Bloody Destinies
	Al-'awwama 70 / Houseboat 70
1986	Al-Tauq wal-aswira / The Necklace and the Bracelet / *aka* The Ring and the Bracelet
1989	Yawm murr, yawm hulw / Bitter Day, Sweet Day
1991	Raghba mutawahesha / Wild Desire

BEYE, Ben Diogaye   Senegal

1947 Dakar, Senegal. He received his early education in Dakar and trained as a journalist. Beye has written scripts and worked with other Senegalese film-makers such as **Diop-Mambéty** and **Thiam**. He worked as an assistant director for television in France and Sweden and directed his first film in 1975.

Filmography

1975	Les princes noirs de Saint-Germain-des-Prés / The Black Princes of Saint-Germain-des-Prés
	Samba-Tali / Le vagabond / The Vagabond
1980	Seye Seyeti *[Wolof]* / Un homme des femmes / A Man, Women
1988	Le train du cœur / Train of the Heart
1991	Le rêve de Latricia / Latricia's Dream

BIVONA, Marcello Tunisia

BIVONA, Marcello   **Tunisia**

5.11.1953 Tunis, Tunisia. He studied art at Brera in Tunisia where he graduated with a diploma in fine art. He studied cinema in Italy. Bivona worked as assistant director to Italian director Peter Del Monte on his film *Piso Pisello* (1981) before making his own directorial début in 1987.

Filmography

1987	Carlotta un antico amore / Charlotte, an Ancient Love
1989	No alla droga / No To Drugs
1990	Niente da fare tutto da fare / Nothing To Be Done, Everything To Be Done
1992	Clandestini nella citta / Clandestines in the City

BLIGNAUT, Johan South Africa

22.2.1953 Benoni, Transvaal, South Africa. He began his career as a stage actor (1974). Since then he has worked extensively in theatre, television and cinema, having written, directed and produced for all three media. He worked with PACT theatre group for three years and then formed his own innovative theatre company which for many years toured political plays throughout South Africa. Blignaut is now an independent film producer and distributor and managing director of Film and Television Group, whose Everis Films has produced such films as the feature *Die posman / The Postman* (1987) and the documentary about African mythology and reptiles, *The Crested Serpent* (1988). He has served as executive producer or producer on nearly twenty feature films for the cinema, including *The Native Who Caused All the Trouble* (**Rensburg**, 1989), *Dark City* (Chris Curling, 1989) *A.W.O.L.* (Neil Sonnekus, 1989) and *Underground* (1990). In 1989 Blignaut founded Showdata, a computerised on-line information and research service for the entertainment industries in southern Africa. He is editor and publisher of the book *Movies Moguls Mavericks: South African Cinema 1979-1991* (1992).

Filmography

1984	Spookstories / Ghost Stories (TV series)
	Mens en dier / People and Animals (TV series)
1985	Mamza
1986	Tojan

BOUAMARI, Mohamed   Algeria

20.1.1941 Sétif, north-eastern Algeria. He received his early education in Sétif and in Tunis. A self-taught film-maker, Bouamari was an immigrant worker in France during Algeria's anti-colonialist war against the French. He returned to Algeria after independence (1962). He worked as an assistant on the film *Rih al-Awras / Le vent des Aurès / Wind of the Aurès* (**Lakhdar-Hamina**, 1966) and made his directorial début in 1969.

Filmography

1969	Conflit / Conflict
1972	Al-Fahham / Le charbonnier / The Charcoal Man
1974	Al-Irth / The Inheritance
1980	Al-Khutwat al-Ula / Premier pas / The First Steps
1982	Al-Rafdh / The Refusal

BOUCHAREB, Rachid   Algeria

1953 Paris, France. He worked for the Société Française de Production Cinématographique (SFPC) as an assistant director. Together with film-maker Jean Bzehat, Bouchareb formed a company to produce his 1991 film *Cheb*.

Filmography

1976	La pièce / The Piece
1977	La chute / The Fall
1978	Le banc / The Bench
1983	Peut-être la mer / Perhaps the Sea
1985	Bâton rouge / Red Baton
1991	Cheb

BOUGHEDIR, Ferid   Tunisia

11.3.1944 Hammam Lif near Tunis, Tunisia. His father was a writer and journalist. Boughedir studied literature at the Université de Rouen and acquired his doctorate on Arab and African cinema from the Université de Paris III (Sorbonne-Nouvelle). He gained experience in film-making by working as assistant director to French director Alain Robbe-Grillet and the Spanish playwright and director Fernando Arrabal. He is one of the best known African film critics, writing for *Jeune Afrique*, and has written many articles and several books on African and Arab cinema history, including *Le cinéma en Afrique et dans le monde* (1984) and *Le cinéma africain de A à Z* (1987). Boughedir has also written or co-written several film scripts, including *Mokhtar* (**Aïcha Sadok Ben**, 1968) and *La mort trouble / Death Is Disturbing* (Claude d'Anna, 1968). He currently teaches cinema at university in Tunis.

Filmography

1964	Riche pour un jour / Rich for a Day (co-dir Mustapha Mourali)
1966	Paris-Tunis
1983	Caméra d'Afrique / African Camera
	Le pique-nique / The Picnic
1984	Cinéma de Carthage / The Cinema of Carthage
1987	Caméra arabe / Arab Camera
1990	Halfaouine / *aka* Child of the Terraces

BOUZID, Nouri   Tunisia

1945 Sfax, Tunisia. He studied at the Institut National des Arts du Spectacle et Techniques de Diffusion (INSAS) in Brussels (grad. 1972). After working as an assistant director on about fifteen films, he directed his first feature film *Rih al-Sadd / L'homme de cendres / Man of Ashes* (1989).

Filmography

1989	Rih al-Sadd / L'homme de cendres / Man of Ashes
1990	Safaih min dhahab / Sabots en or / Gold Leaf / *aka* Golden Hooves

BRIGHT, Simon   Zimbabwe

March 1952 Harare, Zimbabwe. He received his early education in Harare. Bright studied English literature at the University of Cambridge in England and obtained an MA in rural development at the University of Reading. He returned to Zimbabwe after independence in 1980 and made his directorial début seven years later with *Corridors of Freedom*.

Filmography

1987   Corridors of Freedom
1988   Battle of Cuito Cuanavale
1989   Limpopo Line
1990   Mbira Music - Spirit of the People

See also: 134b.

CAMARA, Dansogho Mohamed   Guinea

1945 Guinea. He trained initially as a teacher and worked at Dabadou Primary School in Kankan (1960-64). He acted, produced and directed many plays which were performed mainly in Conakry (1967-70). In 1971 he went to East Germany where he studied cinematography.

Filmography

1975   La métallurgie / Metallurgy
1976   La lourdeur des rendez-vous manqués / The Awkwardness of Wasted
            Meetings
1977   Du donner et du reçevoir / Give and Take
1979   Les traditions orales, les arts africains et le cinéma / Oral Traditions,
            African Art and the Cinema
1983   Ouloukoro
            Le chemin du combattant / The Way of the Warrior
            L'école guinéenne / The Guinean School
            Sere / The Witness

CARDOSO, José António Ribeiro   Mozambique

6.4.1930 Figueira Castelo Rodrigo, Portugal. He emigrated with his parents to Mozambique in 1937. Cardoso studied pharmacy and worked as a pharmacist for over thirty years; he studied cinema by reading specialist and technical books. He joined a group of amateur film-makers in Beira, the capital of Sofala province of Mozambique, and acquired film-making experience by directing 8mm films.

Filmography

1966	O anúncio / The Advert
1968	Raízes / Roots
1969	Pesadelo / Nightmare
1981	Que venham / Let Them Come
	O papagaio / The Parrot
1982	Canta meu irmão, ajuda-me a cantar / Sing, Brother, Help Me To Sing
1987	O vento sopra do norte / The Wind Blows from the North

See also: 130/Ib.

22.4.1941 Portugal. Carvalho initially studied social sciences. His childhood years spent in southern Angola are often the background to his work as a short story writer and poet, particularly in *A decisão da idade / The Judgement of Age* (1976) and *Como se o mundo não tivesse leste / As If There Were No East* (1977). In 1975 he became a naturalised citizen of Angola. Although his output consists predominantly of documentaries, Carvalho has made one feature film (1982).

Filmography

1975	Sou angolano, trabalho com o força / I'm Angolan, I Work Hard
	Geração 50 / Generation 50
	Viriato da Cruz
1976	Uma festa para viver / A Party for Life
1977	Faz a coragem, camarada / Courage, Comrade
	Está tudo sentado no chão / They're All on the Floor
	Como foi como não foi / As It Was, As It Wasn't
	O deserto e os mucubais / The Desert and the Mucubais
1980	Presente angolano, lua da seca menor / Angola Now, In the Moon of a Short Drought (in *Tempo mumuila* film series)
1982	Nelisita
	Balanço do tempo na cena de Angola / Timeshift in Angola
1989	O recado das ilhas / Le message des îles / Message from the Islands

25.5.1959 Catuane, Maputo province, southern Mozambique. In 1977 he joined the Instituto Nacional de Cinema (INC) where he completed a course in film editing. Chabela worked for a period as an assistant editor, then as an editor. He made many short documentaries up to 1979 before making his first film.

Filmography

1979	Assim elas vivem / Such Is Their Life (co-dir Enoque Maté, **Ismaël Marcelino Vuvo**)
1981	O futuro somos nós / We Are the Future
1982	Cidade entre montanhas / Town Between Mountains
	Do gesto tenso a liberdade / From a Nervous Gesture to Freedom
1983	Paraquedismos / Parachuting
1984	A madrugada da vida / The Dawn of Life
1987	Shangara, o desafio / Shangara, the Challenge

See also: 149/lf.

25.1.1926 Alexandria, Egypt. The son of a lawyer, Chahine showed a talent for painting as a child. He was educated at Victoria College and at Alexandria University. In 1946 he went to the United States where he spent two years studying at the Pasadena Playhouse in California. On returning to Egypt (1948), he worked for the Italian documentary director Gianni Vernuccio. Chahine made his first film in 1950 and is widely regarded as one of the most prolific and well-known Egyptian feature film-makers and a major figure in world cinema. *Bab al-Hadid / Cairo Station* (1958), in which Chahine himself took the leading role, was warmly received at the Berlin Film Festival. His 1954 film *Sira' fil wadi / The Blazing Sun* established Omar Sharif as an actor. Chahine left Egypt temporarily and made a film in Lebanon (1965) and one in Spain (1966) before his return. *Iskandariya... leeh? / Alexandria... Why?* won the Special Jury Prize at the 1979 Berlin Film Festival.

Filmography

1950	Baba Amin / Daddy Honest / *aka* Father Amin / *aka* Papa Amin
1951	Ibn al-Nil / Nile Boy / *aka* Son of the Nile
1952	Al-Muharrij al-Kabir / The Great Clown / *aka* The Big Buffoon
1953	Sayedat al-Qitar / The Woman on the Train
	Nisa bila rijal / Women Without Men / *aka* Only Women
1954	Sira' fil wadi / The Blazing Sun / *aka* Struggle in the Valley
	Shaytan al-Sahra / Desert Devil / *aka* Devil in the Desert / *aka* The Demon of the Desert
1956	Sira' fil-mina / Dark Waters / *aka* Struggle in the Port
1957	Inta habibi / My One and Only Love / *aka* You Are My Love
	Wadda' tu hubbak / Farewell My Love / *aka* Goodbye To Your Love
1958	Bab al-Hadid / Cairo Station / *aka* Cairo: Central Station
	Jamileh al-Jazairiyya / Jamila / *aka* Djamila
1959	Hubb lel-abad / Forever Yours / *aka* Yours Forever
1960	Bayna aydik / In Your Hands / *aka* Between Your Hands
1961	Nida al' ushshaq / Lovers' Complaint / *aka* Call of the Lovers
	Rajul fi hayati / A Man In My Life
1963	Al-Nasir Salah al-Din / Saladin
1964	Fajr yawm jadid / Dawn of a New Day
1965	Bayaa' al-Khawatim / The Ring Seller / *aka* The Seller of Rings
1966	Rimal min dhahab / Golden Sands / *aka* Sand of Gold
1968	Al-Nas wal-Nil / Those People of the Nile / *aka* People of the Nile
1969	Al-Ard / The Land
1970	Al-Ikhtiyar / The Choice
1972	Salwa / Salwa, the Girl Who Talked To Cows
1973	Al-'usfur / The Sparrow
1974	Intilak / Forward We Go / *aka* Freedom
1976	'Awdat al-Ibn al-Dhall / The Return of the Prodigal Son
1978	Iskandariya... leeh? / Alexandria... Why?
1982	Hadutha masriyya / An Egyptian Story
1984	Al-Wida'a Bonaparte / Adieu Bonaparte / *aka* Farewell Bonaparte
1986	Al-Yawm al-Sadis / The Sixth Day
1990	Iskandariya, kaman wa kaman / Alexandria Again and Again
1991	Cairo As Told By Yusuf Chahine

See also: 2/lb, 14b, 25/lb, 103/lb, 120b.

CHOUIKH, Mohamed   Algeria

1943 Mostaganem, Algeria. In 1963 he joined a pioneering group of performers which became the Algerian National Theatre. He went to Paris with the company when it presented four plays in Arabic, and subsequently toured throughout Europe. After acting in the film *Fajr al-Mu'adhdhabin / L'aube des damnés / The Dawn of the Damned* (**Rachedi**, 1965), Chouikh was selected to star in the first authentically Algerian film, *Rih al-Awras / Le vent des Aurès / Wind of the Aurès* (**Lakhdar-Hamina**, 1966) and then appeared in the Algerian western *Al-Kharijun 'an al-Qanum / Les hors-la-loi / The Outlaws* (**Farès**, 1968). Subsequently he played parts in *¿* (1969) and *Elise ou la vraie vie / Elise or Real Life* (1970), both directed by Michel Drach, as well as in such films as *Masirat al-Ru'ah / Les nomades / The Nomads* (**Mazif**, 1975). Having also worked in cinema and television as an assistant director and having written two plays, Chouikh soon began to seek opportunities to write and direct his own films.

Filmography

1982   Al-Inqita' / Rupture
1988   Al-Qal'a / The Citadel

CISSÉ, Mahamadou   Mali

1951 Kayes, Mali. He abandoned his studies to join a professional football club. In 1984 he published his first book *La roue de la vie / The Wheel of Life*. Cissé became very interested in cinema and in 1989 released his first film.

Filmography

1989   Falato *[Bambana]* / L'orphelin / The Orphan
1990   Yelema

21.4.1940 Bamako, Mali. Born into a large Muslim family, Cissé is of the Sarakholé ethnic group. His father was a tailor with little time to keep an eye on his many children. Cissé took advantage of his childhood freedom by going to open-air movie theatres. As a result his school performance was affected and eventually he was expelled. The family moved to Dakar in Senegal where Cissé went to secondary school; the family returned to Bamako after the independence of Mali in 1960. He began to organise film screenings and in 1961 was awarded a three-month scholarship to attend a course for projectionists in the Soviet Union. In 1962 he saw a film on the arrest of Zaïre's first prime minister, Patrice Lumumba and the torture he suffered before he died. At that moment Cissé realised the power and influence of the film medium and decided to get involved in film-making. He received a major scholarship to study cinema under Mark Donskoj at VGIK in Moscow (1963-69). On his return to Mali (1969), Cissé was offered a job as director in the film section at the Service Cinématographique du Ministère de l'Information du Mali (SCINFOMA), where he produced several newsreels and documentary films (1970-71). He directed his first fiction film in 1972 and is considered one of Africa's most prominent film-makers.

Filmography

1965	L'homme et les idoles / Man and Idols
1966	Sources d'inspiration / Sources of Inspiration
1968	L'aspirant / The Candidate
1970	Degal à Dialloube / Degal at Dialloube
1971	Fête du Sanké / The Sanké Celebration
1972	Cinq jours d'une vie / Five Days in a Life
1973	Dixième anniversaire de l'OAU / Tenth Anniversary of the OAU
1974	Den muso *[Bambana]* / La jeune fille / The Young Girl / *aka* The Girl
1978	Baara *[Bambana]* / Le travail / Work
	Chanteurs traditionnels des îles seychelles / Traditional Singers of the Seychelles
1982	Finye *[Bambana]* / Le vent / The Wind
1987	Yeelen *[Bambana]* / La lumière / The Light / *aka* Brightness

CONDE, Khalifa   Guinea

Guinea. He trained and worked as a journalist for a period before enrolling at VGIK in Moscow, Russia.

Filmography

1983   Quelques pages de la vie de Toussaint L'Ouverture / Some Pages from
        the Life of Toussaint L'Ouverture (co-dir Daouda Keita)

COSTA, João Manuel Abranches Martins   Mozambique

5.5.1951 Viana do Castelo, Portugal. Costa has lived in Mozambique since November 1951. He attended a three-year course in mechanical engineering in Maputo. He then worked as an illustrator in the faculty of medicine at the Universidade Eduardo Mondlane in Maputo (1972-74). For a short period he was a photojournalist for the magazine *A Voz de Moçambique* and then a photographer for the newspaper *Notícias* (1974-77). In 1977 he enrolled on a course in cinematography at the Instituto Nacional de Cinema (INC). He then began working for the institute as a camera operator and director.

Filmography

1977   Vamos eleger os nossos deputados / Let's Vote for Our Candidates
1978   Vozes livres / Voices of Freedom
1980   2 músicas, 5 meticais
        Obrigado Zimbabwe / Thank You Zimbabwe
        Cinco tiros de mauser / Five Mauser Shots (co-dir **Camillo de Souza**)
1981   Pamberi ne Zimbabwe (co-dir Carlos Henriques)
1982   Ibo, o sangue do silêncio / Ibo, the Blood of Silence (co-dir **Camillo de
        Souza**)
        Cinco vezes mais / Five More Times (co-dir **Camillo de Souza**)
1983   Porque alguma voz são todas as vozes / Why Are Some Voices All
        Voices? (co-dir **Camillo de Souza**)
1984   Acordo de Nkomati / The Nkomati Accord (co-dir **Camillo de Souza**)

See also: 134f.

COSTEL, Herlim Pedro Jorge   Mozambique

21.12.1958 Mocuba in Zambézia province, northern central Mozambique. He attended secondary school in Nampula. In 1979 Costel enrolled at the Universidade Eduardo Mondlane in Maputo. After graduating he worked for Radio Mozambique where he wrote and directed drama and poetry programmes (1980-85). Between 1985 and 1989 he was director of production for Kanemo, a local film production company. Costel formed his own production company, Eco Productions (1989) and has worked as an editor and producer on several films.

Filmography

1991   Building the Future - Street Children

COULIBALY, Mambaye   Mali

2.5.1957 Kayes, western Mali. He received his early education in Mali and has lived in both Mali and France, where he studied cinema under the direction of French anthropologist and film-maker Jean Rouch. He also studied anthropology and ethnology at the Université de Paris (Panthéon-Sorbonne). Coulibaly is also a composer and authority on traditional African music. His début as a director is an animated film.

Filmography

1989   Segu-Janjo [Bambana] / La geste de Ségou / Ségou's Gesture

COULIBALY, Sega   Mali

1950 Dakar, Senegal. He studied in Paris at both the Institut des Hautes Etudes Cinématographiques (IDHEC) and the Conservatoire Libre du Cinéma Français (CLCF).

Filmography

1976	Mogho Dakan *[Bambana]* / Le destin / Destiny
	Rituel de chasse au pays mandingue / Hunting Ritual in Mandingo Country
1978	Kasso den *[Bambana]* / Le prisonnier / The Prisoner

DAMAK, Mohamed   Tunisia

Sfax, Tunisia. He has been very active in the Tunisian Federation of Ciné Clubs and in the Amateur Film-Makers Federation. He was assistant director on several short films before making his own directorial début in 1985.

Filmography

1985   The Cup

DANIELS, Ta   Ghana

1936 Ghana. After secondary school he joined the Gold Coast Film Unit (now Ghana Film Industry Corporation) where he received his initial training in film production (1957). In 1965 he travelled to Poland where he spent six months on a course in Warsaw. He then went to India (1968) where he registered for a three-year course in direction at the National Film and Television Institute of India. He has been an executive of the Ghana Film Industry Corporation since 1983.

Filmography

1991   Aya Minnow

DAO, Moustapha   Burkina Faso

1955 Koudougou, Burkina Faso. He studied photography at the Institut Africain d'Education Cinématographique (INAFEC) in Ouagadougou. Dao then worked as a director for the Société Africaine de Production Cinématographique (CINAFRIC). He has also worked for his country's national television station.

Filmography

1986   A nous la rue / The Road Is Ours
1989   Le neveu du peintre / The Painter's Nephew
1991   L'enfant et le caïman / The Child and the Crocodile

DELGADO, Clarence Thomas   Senegal

1953 Dakar, Senegal. He studied cinema in Algeria and Portugal. Delgado worked as an assistant to **Sembene** and his début feature as a director is an adaptation of one of Sembene's novels.

Filmography

1988   Niiwam

DERKAOUI, Mustapha Abdelkrim   Morocco

1941 Oujda, northern Morocco. After his secondary education he studied theatre in Casablanca and cinema both in Poland and at the Institut des Hautes Etudes Cinématographiques (IDHEC) in Paris, where he graduated with a diploma in film production. He returned to Morocco to work initially with fellow film-maker **Reggab** and then independently.

Filmography

1964   Les quatre murs / The Four Walls
1966   Amghar
1969   Etats-généraux du cinéma / The Summit Meeting on the Cinema
1974   De quelques événements sans signification / About Some Events Without
           Significance
1979   Les cendres du clos / The Cinders of the Yard (co-dir **Mohamed Reggab**)
1982   Ayyam Shehrezad al-Jamila / Les beaux jours de Schéhérazade / The
           Beautiful Days of Scheherazade

See also: 116/IIb, 116/IIf.

DIA-MOUKOURI, Urbain   Cameroon

1935 Douala, Cameroon. He studied cinema at the Conservatoire Libre du Cinéma Français (CLCF) in Paris and made his début in 1965. All his films have been features.

Filmography

1965	Point de vue 1 / Point of View 1
1966	Il était une fois deux frères / Once Upon a Time There Were Two Brothers
1968	La fleur dans le sang / The Flower in the Blood
1969	Les coucous / Cuckoos
1973	Soleil d'avril / April Sunshine
1982	La brûlure / The Burn
1983	Le veinard / The Lucky Person

DIABATE, Idriss   Ivory Coast

13.9.1948 Duékoué, western Ivory Coast. He studied at the Université de Paris XIII (Paris-Nord) (grad. 1976). Since 1982 he has been teaching audio visual studies at the National Institute of Art in Abidjan, Ivory Coast. He has made many documentaries on video and on Super 8.

Filmography

1985	La face cachée du Centre Beaubourg / The Hidden Face of the Beaubourg Centre
1986	Attieke manioc / Cassave
1988	Le processus de fabrication du tam tam / *aka* Tam Tam / The Making of the Tam-Tam
	Une musicienne ivoirienne Zele de Papara / Ivory Coast Musician: Zele de Papara
1989	Banane plantain une grosse légume / Mr Plantain, the Big Wig
1991	Dans le canari des plantes / In the Tub of Plants
	Vous avez dit peinture / You Said Painting

DIABATE, Sidy   Burkina Faso

1950 Burkina Faso. He studied economics at university. He worked as assistant director on **Drabo's** two films *Nieba* (1986) and *Ta Donna* (1990) and also assisted **Sissoko** on *Finzan* (1989). Diabate is also an accomplished actor.

Filmography

1981/6   Veillée à Bolongue / Evening at Bolongue

DIAKATE, Moussa Kemoko   Guinea

10.9.1940 Mamou, Guinea. He received his primary and secondary education in Mamou and studied drama in West Germany. He then acted in a number of films, including *Le sergent Bakary Woolen / Sergeant Bakary Woolen* (**Akin**, 1966) and *Hier, aujourd'hui, demain / Yesterday, Today, Tomorrow* (Costa Diagne, 1968). He co-directed his first feature film *Hirde Dyama* in 1971. Diakate was recognised as a talented film-maker at the 1973 Festival Panafricain du Cinéma de Ouagadougou (FESPACO) for *Hommage à Kwame Nkrumah / Homage to Kwame Nkrumah* (1972), his film on the first leader of independent Ghana. All his films have been documentaries except the most recent.

Filmography

1969   Riziculture dans le Bagata / Rice-Growing in Bagata
       Centre caféier de Nzerékoré / Coffee-Shrub Centre in Nzerékoré
       Journal de la campagne agricole / A Journal of the Agricultural
          Countryside
1971   Hirde Dyama (co-dir G Jeutz)
       Le 14 mai 1970 / 14th of May 1970
1972   Hommage à Kwame Nkrumah / Homage to Kwame Nkrumah
       Les funérailles de Kwame Nkrumah / The Funeral of Kwame Nkrumah
1975   L'université à la campagne / University in the Countryside
1978   Hafia, triple champion d'Afrique / Hafia, Africa's Three Times Champion
       Le sport en Guinée / Sport in Guinea
       Sommet de Monrovia / The Monrovia Summit
1982   Naïtou l'orpheline / Naïtou, the Orphan Girl

DIALLO, Ahmed   Senegal

4.2.1952 Dakar, Senegal. He studied drama and began working in the cinema as an assistant director on several Senegalese films before making his début in 1986.

Filmography

1986   Fokuwaay
1991   Boxulmaleen *[Wolof]* / L'an...fer / Iron Year

DIENTA, Kalifa   Mali

1940 Macina, central Mali. After attending schools in Macina and Bamako, Dienta worked at various jobs. He received a scholarship to study film in Moscow. On his return he directed his first film *L'épargne en milieu rural / Saving in a Rural Environment* (1978).

Filmography

1978   L'épargne en milieu rural / Saving in a Rural Environment
1980   A Banna *[Bambana]* / It's All Over

DIKONGUE-PIPA, Jean-Pierre   Cameroon

20.10.1940 Douala, Cameroon. He spent his early years watching the films of Charlie Chaplin at local movie theatres. His nationalist father vigorously opposed French colonial rule in Cameroon and was arrested and deported. The young Dikongue-Pipa spent his childhood with his mother. At the age of sixteen he formed a theatre troupe, the Jeunesse Artistique club. He wrote many plays which were performed by friends and schoolmates. He was later sent to France where he studied electrical engineering and was also a professional footballer (1961-62). In 1962 Dikongue-Pipa enrolled at the Conservatoire Libre du Cinéma Français (CLCF) in Paris where he trained for two years. He then worked in various odd jobs and with the help of the French Ministry of Co-operation, who gave him film stock, he shot three short documentaries (1965-66). On his return to Cameroon (1966), he set up a new theatre troupe, l'Avant-Garde Africaine and staged many plays (1966-67). In 1974, again with financial support from the Ministry of Co-operation, as well as with personal loans and help from his friends and actors from his company who offered to work for little or no pay, Dikongue-Pipa began shooting his first feature-length film *Muna Moto / L'enfant de l'autre / Somebody Else's Child*. It was screened widely and praised at international festivals.

Filmography

1965	Un simple / Down to Earth
1966	Les cornes / The Horns
	Rendez-moi mon père / Give Me Back My Father
1974	Muna Moto / L'enfant de l'autre / Somebody Else's Child
1978	Le prix de la liberté / The Price of Freedom
1980	Kpa Kum
1981	Music and Music
1982	Histoires drôles, drôles de gens / Funny Stories, Funny People
1983	Badyaga / Courte maladie / Brief Illness
1983/5	La cicatrice / The Scar
1984	Foire aux livres à Harare / Book Fair in Harare

DIOP, David Ika   Senegal

Dakar, Senegal. He is the son of the famous Senegalese poet David Mandessi Diop, who disappeared in an air disaster in 1960. Diop made his début film *Poète de l'amour / Poet of Love* (1985) in memory of his father.

Filmography

1985   Poète de l'amour / Poet of Love

DIOP, Maguette   Senegal

1948 Dakar, Senegal. He studied cinema at the Conservatoire Libre du Cinéma Français (CLCF) in Paris and made his directorial début in 1975.

Filmography

1975   Les fauves en liberté / Wild Animals Roaming Free
1980   Le fils de qui? / Whose Son?
1986   N'Diguel et Touba / N'Diguel and Touba

DIOP, Mustapha   Niger

4.4.1945 Cotonou, Dahomey (now Benin). His mother was from Dahomey and his father was Malian. Diop completed his primary education in Mali and his secondary studies in Niger. He obtained his first degree in modern literature at the Université de Paris (1968). His studies in literature were continued at the universities of Abidjan (Ivory Coast) and Ouagadougou (Burkina Faso). In 1975 he registered at Institut des Hautes Etudes Cinématographiques (IDHEC) in Paris, where he graduated with diplomas in both editing and production (1978). Between 1979 and 1984 he worked as a producer for Niger television. Diop produced and directed his first film *Synapse* in 1974. All his films have been features.

Filmography

1974	Synapse
1979	Bouba
1980	La tomate / The Tomato
1982	Le médecin de Gafiré / Gafiré's Doctor
1989	Mamy Wata

See also: 25/IIb.

DIOP-MAMBÉTY, Djibril   Senegal

1945 Dakar, Senegal. He is of Wolof origin and Muslim extraction. Since his youth he has been interested in the theatre. After secondary school he studied drama for two years in Dakar and then worked as a stage actor-director at the Théâtre Daniel Sorano there. Diop-Mambéty made his début as a cinema director with the first comic African film *Contrast City* (1968). He has also acted in various Italian films. *Parlons, grand-mère / Let's Talk, Granny* is about the making of *Yaaba* (**Idrissa Ouedraogo**, 1989).

Filmography

1968	Contrast City / *aka* A City of Contrasts
1970	Badou Boy (also earlier version 1966)
1973	Touki-bouki *[Wolof]* / Le voyage de l'hyène / The Hyena's Journey
1989	Parlons, grand-mère / Let's Talk, Granny
1991	Hyènes / Hyenas

See also: 30b, 36/IIb.

DJEDAIET, Mahmoud   Algeria

Algeria. He studied at the Conservatoire Libre du Cinéma Français (CLCF) in France. He has to his credit several short films, including television productions. Djedaiet has participated in the shooting of several films, including *Mohamed the Messenger of God* (1975) and *El Rissala / The Message* (1987).

Filmography

1984   Zone 5
1985   The Real and Rose Water

DJIM, Mamadou Kola   Burkina Faso

27.1.1940 Ouagadougou, Burkina Faso. He worked as a primary school teacher before enrolling at the Conservatoire Libre du Cinéma Français (CLCF) in Paris, where he studied film-making. He is a founder member of both the Ouagadougou Cinema Club and the Association of Film-Makers in Burkina Faso. For a period he was the editor of the magazine *Faces of Africa* before directing his first film *Le sang des parias / The Blood of the Pariahs* in 1971.

Filmography

1971   Le sang des parias / The Blood of the Pariahs
1982   Cissin, cinq ans plus tard / Cissin, Five Years Later (co-dir Maurice
          Bulbulian)
1985   Kognini *[Dyula]*
1990   Les étrangers / The Strangers

DONG, Pierre-Marie   Gabon

1945 Libreville, Gabon. After secondary school he went to Paris to study film-making at the Institut des Hautes Etudes Cinématographiques (IDHEC). Dong returned to Gabon after graduation and started working for national television in Libreville. During this period he began to make his own films. He also acted in several films, including *Il était une fois Libreville / Once Upon a Time Libreville* (**Auge**, 1974). Dong was later appointed general manager of Gabonese television and is currently head of Organisme du Cinéma Gabonais, the Gabonese film bureau. *Obali* and *Ayouma* are both adaptations of stories by Joséphine Bongo, the wife of President Bongo.

Filmography

1969	Carrefour humain / Human Crossroads
	Gabon, pays de contraste / Gabon, a Country of Contrasts
1970	Lésigny
1971	Sur le sentier du requiem / En Route to the Requiem
1972	Identité / Identity
1976	Obali (co-dir **Charles Mensah**)
1977	Ayouma (co-dir **Charles Mensah**)
1978	Demain, un jour nouveau / Tomorrow Is Another New Day

See also: 99/IIf, 118/Ib.

DOSSO, Moussa   Ivory Coast

1946 Lakota, Ivory Coast. He studied cinema at the Université de Paris VIII.

Filmography

1979	Le koussi / The Koussi
1982	Dalokan / La parole donnée / The Promise

DOUKOURE, Cheik   Guinea

1943 Kankan, Guinea. After completing his studies in Conakry, Doukoure moved to Paris (1964). He enrolled at the Université de Paris (Panthéon-Sorbonne) and graduated with a diploma in 1968. He then registered at the Cours Simon (Institut d'Art Dramatique) and studied acting at the Conservatoire Libre du Cinéma Français (CLCF). He has acted in several films and also for the stage.

Filmography

1988	Baro, le lac sacré / Baro, the Sacred Lake
1991	Blanc d'ébène / Ebony White

DRABO, Adama   Mali

1948 Bamako, Mali. He was a village schoolteacher for many years (1968-79). In his spare time Drabo wrote plays and studied cinema at the Centre National de Production Cinématographique (CNPC) in Bamako. He worked as an assistant to **Sissoko** on his films *Nyamanton / La leçon des ordures / Lessons from the Garbage* (1986) and *Finzan* (1989).

Filmography

1986	Nieba: la journée d'une paysanne / Nieba, A Peasant's Day
1990	Ta Donna *[Bambana]* / Fire

See also: 53/Ib.

DUPARC, Henri

25.12.1941 Forécariah, south-western Guinea. After primary school in Forécariah and secondary school in Kindia, his father sent him to Paris where he completed his secondary education. Whilst in Paris Duparc developed his interest in the cinema and spent most of his spare time at the Cinémathèque Française. In 1962 he was awarded a scholarship to study film-making in Belgrade. He returned to Paris and worked briefly as a bank clerk before enrolling at the Institut des Hautes Etudes Cinématographiques (IDHEC). He also acted in several films, including *Concerto pour un exil / Concerto For an Exile* (**Ecaré**, 1968) and returned to the Ivory Coast in 1968. Duparc made several short documentaries before his début feature *Mouna ou le rêve d'un artiste / Mouna, or An Artist's Dream* (1969).

Filmography

1967	Obs... (uncompleted)
1968	Récolte du coton / Growing Cotton
	Achetez ivoirien / Buy Ivory Coast Products
1969	Mouna ou le rêve d'un artiste / Mouna, or An Artist's Dream
	Profil ivoirien / Ivory Coast Profile
	Tam-tam ivoirien / Ivory Coast Drum
1970	J'ai dix ans / I Am Ten Years Old
	Carnet de voyage / A Traveller's Notes
1972	Abusuan / La famille / The Family
1976	Les racines de la vie / The Roots of Life
1977	L'herbe sauvage / Weeds / *aka* Wild Grass
1987	J'ai choisi de vivre / I've Chosen Life
	Aya
1988	Bal poussière / Dancing In the Dust
1990	Le sixième doigt / The Sixth Finger

ECARÉ, Désiré

15.4.1939 Treichville, a district of Abidjan, Ivory Coast. He completed both his primary and secondary schooling at Catholic educational institutions. Ecaré then studied acting and the theatre at the Centre d'Art Dramatique in Abidjan. He won a scholarship from the Ivory Coast government to continue his drama studies in France. In 1961 he enrolled at the Centre d'Art Dramatique de la rue Blanche (grad. 1963). In 1964 he began studying film-making at the Institut des Hautes Etudes Cinématographiques (IDHEC) in Paris (grad. 1966). He subsequently formed his own production company, Les Films de la Lagune, and his first two films were made in France. In 1972 he returned to the Ivory Coast and worked at the Ministry of Tourism but left to continue his film-making career.

Filmography

1968	Concerto pour un exil / Concerto For an Exile
1970	A nous deux, France / *aka* Femme noire, femme nue / It's Up To Us, France
1985	Visages de femmes / Faces of Women / *aka* Women's Faces
1990	L'Afrique à nous deux / Africa, Here I Come

See also: 25/IIb, 61b.

FADIKA, Kramo-Lanciné

1948 Danané, western Ivory Coast. He was born into a large Muslim family. After completing his schooling in Bingerville (1969), Fadika enrolled at the Université de Côte d'Ivoire in Abidjan to study modern literature (grad. 1971). He went to Paris immediately after graduation and studied at the Ecole Nationale Louis Lumière (1971-74). Fadika returned to Abidjan (1975) and worked at the Office National de la Promotion Rurale, a government body responsible for rural development. He produced several didactic documentaries on health, agriculture and education. In this period he began to shoot his first feature film *Djeli, conte d'aujourd'hui / Djeli, a Story of Today* (1981).

Filmography

1981	Djeli, conte d'aujourd'hui / Djeli, a Story of Today

See also: 84/IIb.

FARÈS, Tewfik   Algeria

27.10.1937 Bordj-Bou-Arréridj, north-eastern Algeria. He worked on several documentaries before making his début with the first Algerian western (1968).

Filmography

1968   Al-Kharijun 'ala al-Qanum / Les hors-la-loi / The Outlaws

See also: 45/Ib.

FAYE, Safi   Senegal

1943 Dakar, Senegal. Faye is one of twenty children of a polygamous village chief of the Serer ethnic group. She attended primary school in Rufisque. Later she trained to be a teacher and whilst doing so (1963) became involved with various cultural events taking place in Dakar. Through one of these festivals she met French film-maker Jean Rouch who encouraged her interest in film-making. She later appeared in a few of Rouch's films, including *Petit à petit / Little by Little* (1970). Faye enrolled to study ethnology at the Ecole Pratique des Hautes Etudes in Paris and subsequently (1972) at the Ecole Nationale Louis Lumière to study film-making. She worked at several odd jobs to support herself and with her savings managed to make her first short film *La passante / The Passerby* (1972/5) whilst a student. Her first full-length film *Kaddu beykat / Lettre paysanne / Letter To My Village*, which she began in 1972, was released in 1975 and won many international festival awards.

Filmography

1972/5   La passante / The Passerby
1973   Revanche / Revenge
1975   Kaddu beykat *[Serer]* / Lettre paysanne / Letter To My Village / *aka* Letter
             from My Village / *aka* Peasant Letter
1979   Goob na nu / The Harvest Is In
             Fad'jal *[Serer]* / Come and Work
1979/83 3 ans 5 mois / 3 Years 5 Months
1980   As Women See It?
1981   Les âmes au soleil / Souls Under the Sun
             Man Sa Yay *[Wolof]* / Moi, ta mère / I, Your Mother
1982   Selbé et tant d'autres / Selbé and So Many Others
1984   Ambassades nourricières / Food Missions
1991   Mossane

FERHATI, Jillali   Morocco

1948 Khemisset, Morocco. He lived in France for ten years and studied literature and sociology in Paris. Ferhati is also an actor and theatre producer. He made two short films before making his feature début *La brèche dans le mur / The Gap in the Wall* (1978). Several of his films have been presented at the Cannes Film Festival.

Filmography

1973	Carom
1974	Bonjour madame
1978	La brèche dans le mur / The Gap in the Wall
1981	'Arais min qasab / Poupées de roseau / Reed Dolls
1991	La plage des enfants perdus / The Beach of Lost Children

FILA, David Pierre   Congo

18.6.1954 Brazzaville, Congo. He attended the Institut Universitaire de Technologie (IUT) at Talence, Bordeaux in France (1979-81). In 1982 he enrolled at the Ecole Nationale Louis Lumière where he completed a course in film production (1983). All his films have been documentaries.

Filmography

1985	Litoro / Le masque du sorcier / The Mask of the Sorcerer
1986	La vie dans la forêt / Life in the Forest
	Les lépreux, agents du développement / Lepers, Agents of Development
1987	Amadou, fabricant de mallettes / Amadou, Maker of Small Suitcases
	Les fondeurs d'aluminium / The Aluminium Casters
	FESPACO, je t'aime / FESPACO, I Love You
1988	Un autre demain / Another Tomorrow
1991	L'homme mémoires / Man of Memories
	Biks
	Le dernier des Babingas / The Last of the Babingas
1992	Tala Tala

FORD, Abiyi   Ethiopia

1935 Addis Ababa, Ethiopia. He has an MFA in film studies from Columbia University in New York. Ford is currently professor of film and mass communication in the department of radio, film and television at Howard University in Washington.

Filmography

1969　First Panafrican Film Festival
1983　50 Years of Painting: Lois Mailou Jones

FORJAZ, Moira   Mozambique

1942 Zimbabwe. She went to South Africa where she enrolled at art school and graduated with a degree in fine art. Forjaz then taught for a while in Swaziland. Returning to Mozambique, she started working as a freelance photojournalist and for the Agência de Informação de Moçambique / Mozambican Information Agency (AIM). She initially became involved in film-making as an assistant editor and editor respectively on the films *Mueda, memória e massacre / Mueda, Memory and Massacre* (1979) and *Ópera do malandro / The Rogue's Opera* (1986), both by the Mozambican film-maker **Guerra**. She also worked as assistant director on the full-length documentary *Música de Moçambique! / The Music of Mozambique* (José Fontseca, 1980) and made her own directorial début in the following year. Both her films to date are documentaries.

Filmography

1981　Um dia numa aldeia comunal / A Day In a Commune
　　　Mineiro Moçambicano / Mozambican Miner

FUBE, Fombe Margaret   Cameroon

12.11.1960 Bafut, north-western Cameroon. She studied at university in Cameroon (grad. 1984). She then took a course in television production at the Yaoundé Television Training Centre in Cameroon (1986-87). After graduation Fube started to work for Cameroonian television where she has been a producer and director of several documentary programmes.

Filmography

1987	Catching Up With School
1989	Pavillon écran / Screen Pavilion
	Cocktail aux décibels / Decibel Cocktail
	Portraits de femmes / Ladies World / *aka* Portraits of Women

GAMBA, Sao   Kenya

3.6.1940 Siaya, Kenya. In 1964 he went to Poland and enrolled at Łódź Film School where he took courses in production and cinematography. After completing his studies (1970), he travelled to Uganda and worked for Ugandan Television (UTV) as a cameraman and producer. Gamba then joined the Voice of Kenya Film Production Unit as a scriptwriter and producer/director (1973-81); in this period he made several documentary films. In 1981 he worked at Kenya Film Corporation as a production manager.

Filmography

1972	The Nine Nations
	The 366 Days
1973	Uganda's Economic War
1975	Maashoi Massae O'l
1976	Watering of the Nation
1977	Waters of Mombasa
	FESTAC 77
1978	Burning Spear
1979	Nyayo Era
	Straws in a Beer Pot
1982	Shadows of the Past
1986	Kolormask / Colour Mask

GAMBOA, Zeze   Angola

1955 Luanda, Angola. After secondary school he worked for Angolan television as a director and sound engineer on several documentary programmes. He left Angola for Paris where he studied sound recording (1982-86). He made his directorial début in 1991.

Filmography

1991   Mopiopio, le souffle d'Angola / Mopiopio, Breath of Angola

GANDA, Oumarou   Niger

1935 Niamey, Niger; died 1.1.1981. Ganda was born into a family of storytellers. He was of Djerma origin and Muslim extraction. After primary school he was conscripted into the French army (Niger was at that time a French colony). He received his training in Niamey and later was stationed in Mali and then sent to fight with French troops against the Indochinese Freedom Fighters (1953-55). After the French defeat (1955) Ganda was discharged and sent back to Niger where he had problems in readjusting. He went to the Ivory Coast where he came into contact with the French ethnologist and film-maker Jean Rouch who introduced him to the cinema. Without having had any acting training, Ganda was asked by Rouch to play the part of an unemployed army veteran in the film *Moi, un noir / I Am Black* (1958). In 1962 Ganda assisted in the production of another Rouch film, *Rose et Landry / Rose and Landry*. After having acquired basic film training in Niamey, Ganda worked as an assistant director in the film department at the French Cultural Centre in Niamey. He later entered a scriptwriting competition and won the £3000 first prize for the best film project. With this money he managed to shoot his first film *Cabascabo* (1968). With **Alassane** Ganda is considered a pioneer of Niger cinema.

Filmography

1968   Cabascabo *[Djerma]*
1970   Le wazzou polygame
1973   Saïtane
1977   Cock, Cock, Cock
1980   L'exilé / The Exiled
        Le Niger au festival de Carthage / Niger at the Carthage Festival

See also: 15b, 84/Ib.

GENINI, Izza   Morocco

1942 Morocco. She studied at the Université de Paris in France. Genini has produced and co-produced films for several film-makers, including *Ablakon* (**Gnoan**, 1984) and *Hadda* (Mohamed Aboulouakar, 1986). She made her own directorial début in 1988 with *Louanges / Praise*.

Filmography

1988	Louanges / Praise
	Rythmes de Marrakesh / Rhythms of Marrakesh
1989	Malhoune
1990	Gnaouas
1991	Moussem

GERIMA, Haïlé   Ethiopia

4.3.1946 Gondar, north-western Ethiopia. His father was a playwright, teacher and historian. As an adolescent Gerima worked as a ticket sales boy at the local movie theatre in his spare time from school. After secondary school he went to Addis Ababa to study drama and to the United States (1967) where he studied acting at the Goodman School of Drama in Chicago. He then moved to the University of California at Los Angeles (UCLA) to study film-making (grad. 1975). Gerima spent some of his time writing plays, including *Chief* (1969-70) and *Awful Pit* (1970-71). In 1971 he made his first short film *Hour Glass*. With the exception of *Mirt sost shi amet / Harvest 3000 Years* (1975), shot in his home country, all his films have been made in the United States. He has taught film-making at Howard University in Washington.

Filmography

1971	Hour Glass
1972	Child of Resistance
1975	Mirt sost shi amet *[Amharic]* / Harvest 3000 Years
1976	Bush Mama
1981	Wilmington 10 - USA 10 000
	Ashes and Embers
1985	After Winter: Sterling Brown
1991	Nunu

GHALEM, Ali   Algeria

20.9.1943 Constantine, north-eastern Algeria. Ghalem is a self-taught film-maker and also well-known as a comedian. He worked as an assistant director on several films in France before releasing his first film *Maktoub / Written* in 1975.

Filmography

1975	Maktoub / Written
1977	L'autre France / The Other France
1982	Une femme pour mon fils / A Wife for My Son

GNOAN, M'bala Roger   Ivory Coast

1943 Grand Bassam, Ivory Coast. He received his training in cinema at the Conservatoire Libre du Cinéma Français in Paris and also completed further studies in Sweden. Most of his films are features.

Filmography

1970	Koundoum
1971	La biche / The Hind
1972	Amanié / Quelles sont les nouvelles? / What's the News?
1974	Gboundo
1975	Le chapeau / The Hat
1984	Ablakon
1988	Bouka

See also: 68/lb.

13.12.1949 Cadique, Guinea-Bissau. He attended a course in cinematography at the Institute of Cuban Art under the direction of Santiago Alvarez. He qualified as a cameraman and director of photography (1972). Gomes started working for television with the late Senegalese film director and historian **Vieyra**. In June 1973 he made his first news film about the second congress of PAIGC (African Party for the Independence of Portuguese Guinea and Cape Verde), a political party fighting to end Portuguese rule. He became assistant director at the National Film Institute of Guinea-Bissau (1978). With Swedish director Leyla Tengroth he acted as cameraman on the television documentary *Bistånd / Aid* (1982). Between 1980 and 1982 he offered his services frequently during the conferences between the non-aligned countries and the OAU (Organisation of African Unity). In 1983 he began work on *Mortu nega*, the first full-length feature film produced in Guinea-Bissau and released in 1988. 'Mortu nega' is the name for 'the one whom death has rejected', a child who survives all his still-born brothers. It is a re-evocation of the war of liberation, after five centuries of Portuguese colonial domination, but is also the personal story of a woman who is fighting for the cause.

Filmography

1975	Encontro dos cinco ministros da educação dos países africanos de expressão oficial portuguesa / Meeting of the Five Ministries of Education of the Portuguese-Speaking African Countries
1976	O regresso do Cabral / The Return of Cabral (co-dir Sana Na N'Hada)
1977	A reconstrução / Reconstruction (co-dir Sergio Spina)
1978	Anos no oca luta / Years of Empty Struggle (co-dir Sana Na N'Hada)
1988	Mortu nega / Those Whom Death Refused
1991	Udju azul di Yonta / Les yeux bleus de Yonta / Blue Eyes of Yonta

2.5.1943 Constantine, north-eastern Algeria. He studied design and painting and also received training in fine arts in Constantine. On graduation he had already established himself as a director of photography. He has also produced a number of documentary films for Algerian television.

Filmography

1962	Les chantiers populaires de reboisement / Popular Reforestation Programmes
1963	Plus d'hommes agenouillés / More Kneeling Men
	Dimanche pour l'Algérie / Sunday for Algeria
1964	Problèmes de la jeunesse / Problems of Youth
	Peuple en marche / People on the March
1966	Retour des cendres de l'Emir / Return of the Emir's Ashes
1967	A ciel ouvert / In the Open Air
1976	Et la femme sahraouie? / The Plight of the Saharan Women
1982	Option recherche scientifique / Scientific Research Option
1983	Conseil national palestinien / Palestinian National Council

GUERRA, Ruy   Mozambique

22.8.1931 Lourenço Marques (now Maputo), Mozambique. He was educated in Portugal and Mozambique and studied film at the Institut des Hautes Etudes Cinématographiques (IDHEC) in Paris (grad. 1954). Guerra worked at the Théâtre National Populaire in Paris and was an assistant director on films by French directors Patrice Dally, Jean Delannoy and Georges Rouquier (1956-57). He spent a period in Brazil (1958-67) and made two uncompleted films. After the independence of Mozambique (1975) he returned to help form a national film industry. He has also appeared as an actor in several films, including a main role in *Aguirre, der Zorn Göttes / Aguirre, Wrath of God* (Werner Herzog, 1972).

Filmography

1954	Les hommes et les autres / The Men and the Others
1962	Os cafajestes / The Hustlers / *aka* The Unscrupulous Ones
1964	Os fuzis / The Guns
1969	Sweet Hunters
1970	Os deuses e os mortos / The Gods and the Dead
1977	A queda / The Fall (co-dir Nelson Xavier)
1979	Mueda, memória e massacre / Mueda, Memory and Massacre
1982	Erendira
1986	Ópera do malandro / The Rogue's Opera
1988	Fábula de la bella palomera / Fable of the Beautiful Pigeon Fancier

See also: 65/IIb.

GUEYE, Galdino Ibrahima   Senegal

1945 St Louis, Senegal. He won a scholarship to study cinema in Stockholm, Sweden.

Filmography

1971	Le racisme en Suède / Racism in Sweden
	Le roi maola / The Maola King

1936 Garkida, Gongola State, Nigeria. He received his primary education in Garkida and competed his schooling at Barewa College. Halilu worked briefly as a civil servant for the Ministry of Information in northern Nigeria. When the Film Unit was established there (1955) he accepted an appointment as an assistant producer. In 1959 he won a scholarship to further his studies and chose to study cinematography. He went to London where he spent a few months with the Overseas Film and Television Centre as well as the Shell Film Unit where he studied scriptwriting and editing. After working in Rome for Italian radio and television he returned to Nigeria to work for the Film Unit. He has made several documentaries; in 1977 he wrote and directed his first feature film *Shehu Umar*. Halilu makes many of his films in the Hausa language.

Filmography

1955	It Pays to Care
1958	Hausa Village
1959	Northern Horizon
1960	Durbar Day
	Giant in the Sun
1962	Eye Care
1963	Rinderpest
1965	Welcome Change
1967	Tourist Delight
	Back to the Land
1974	Pride of the Nation
1977	Black Heritage
	Child Bride
	Shehu Umar *[Hausa]*
1978	Kanta of Kebbi
1981	Moment of Truth

HAMEDI, Mwana Mboyo   Zaïre

1943 Kasongo, Zaïre. He trained as a journalist and spent several years reporting for international news publications. Hamedi studied cinema at the Institut des Hautes Etudes Cinématographiques (IDHEC) in Paris.

Filmography

1971	CFL pour la voie nationale / CFL For the National Road
1972	Le congrès de l'authenticité / The Congress of Authenticity
1973	James Brown
	Tabu Ley tel qu'en lui-même / The Truth About Tabu Ley
1975	CMZ Compagnie Maritime Zaïroise / CMZ Zaïrean Maritime Company
	Fikin

HESSE, Chris   Ghana

29.8.1932 Ghana. After completing his secondary education Hesse, joined the Ghana Film Industry Corporation as a trainee. In 1957 he was appointed an assistant cameraman and by 1963 had become senior cameraman. He studied cinema in various countries, including Poland where he was awarded a diploma in cinematography, and France where he graduated with a diploma in film production techniques. On his return to Ghana Hesse rejoined the Ghana Film Industry Corporation as head of the news department, where he produced several newsreels, advertising films and short documentaries.

Filmography *(dates unknown)*

The Birth of OAU
Voice of Peace
Independence of Togo
Dipo / Puberty Rites
Books for All
Solidarity in Struggle

HILOU, André Demba   Burkina Faso

1950 Burkina Faso. After secondary schooling in Ouagadougou, Hilou went to Germany where he studied film. He also took further courses in cinema at the Société Africaine de Production Cinématographique (CINAFRIC). For a period he was head of the audio visual department at the Ministère de la Santé et de l'Action Sociale du Burkina Faso. He assisted in the production of numerous films, including *Pawéogo* (**Sanou**, 1982). He has directed videos about hospital hygiene and also documentaries on urban development in Burkina Faso.

Filmography

1984   Salubrité en ville / Keeping the Town Clean

Full name: Abid Mohamed Medoun Hondo.   4.5.1936 Atar, Adrar region, western Mauritania. His mother was Mauritanian and his father Senegalese. At the age of eighteen he went to Rabat to train as a cook (1954-58). He then left for France and did several odd jobs in Paris, including fruit picker, dock worker and waiter, and worked as a cook in a restaurant in Marseille. Hondo began attending drama courses run by the French actress Françoise Rosay (1965). After many attempts to get satisfactory roles, he left the French theatre to form his own theatre ensemble, Shango, consisting of his African and West Indian friends (1966). With Hondo as stage director the company produced many works by African, Afro-American and South American writers; it later joined with another theatre company, Les Griots. Hondo also acted in various television and stage plays and worked as an extra in several films, including *Un homme de trop / Shock Troops* (Costa-Gavras, 1967) and *A Walk With Love and Death* (John Huston, 1969). From 1967 Hondo began to work behind the camera as an assistant director on various films, before making his directorial début (1969). Since then he has made all his films in exile. He established his Paris film company Les Films Soleil O in 1969.

Filmography

1969	Balade aux sources / Ballad to the Sources
	Partout ou peut-être nulle part / Everywhere, Nowhere Maybe
	Soleil O / O Sun
1973	Les bicots-nègres, vos voisins / Arabs and Niggers, Your Neighbours / *aka* The Black Wogs Your Neighbours
1975	Sahel la faim pourquoi? / The World's Hunger (co-dir Théo Robichet)
1977	Nous aurons toute la mort pour dormir / We'll Sleep When We Die / *aka* We Have the Whole of Death for Sleeping
1979	Polisario, un peuple en armes / Polisario, a People in Arms
	Les nègres marrons de la liberté / West Indies
1986	Sarraounia

KABA, Alkaly Mali

KABA, Alkaly   Mali

1936 Bamako, Mali. He trained as a teacher in Lyons, France. On his return to Mali, Kaba taught for a few years and also wrote a number of books, including *Die In Order To Live* and *Tales from Black Africa*, both of which won prizes. He studied cinema at the National Film Board of Canada in Montreal (1972-76).

Filmography

1972	Wandyalanka *[Bamana]*
1974	Wallanda / The Lesson
1976	Wamba *[Bamana]* / Entre l'eau et le feu / Between Water and Fire
	Chemin de fer au Mali / The National Railway in Mali
1978	Structure de la société malienne / Mali's Social Structure

23.4.1951 Bobo Dioulasso, Burkina Faso. He was born into a large Catholic family of Burkina Faso's main ethnic group, the Mossi. He was educated at a primary school in Ouagadougou and at a secondary boarding school near Bobo Dioulasso. He then studied at the Centre d'Etudes Supérieures d'Histoire d'Ouagadougou (1970-72) and in Paris where he obtained an MA in history (1972-74). In Paris he began to take a serious interest in cinema and in 1974 enrolled at the Ecole Supérieure d'Etudes Cinématographiques (ESEC) to study cinematography. Returning to Burkina Faso, he was appointed director of the Centre National du Cinéma (CNC) and also began teaching at the Institut Africain d'Education Cinématographique (INAFEC) in Ouagadougou. After making several documentaries, Kaboré made his début feature (1982). In 1985 he was appointed general secretary of the Fédération Panafricaine des Cinéastes (FEPACI), an organisation established to promote a united front amongst all African film-makers in the interests of cultural co-operation.

Filmography

1977   Je reviens de Bokin / I Come From Bokin / *aka* I'm Coming Back From
        Bokin
1978   Stockez et conservez les grains / Store and Conserve the Grain
1979   Regard sur le VIème FESPACO / A Look at the 6th FESPACO
1980   Utilisation des énergies nouvelles en milieu rural / The Use of New Energy
        in Rural Areas
1982   Wend Kuuni *[Moore]* / Le don de Dieu / Wend Kuuni, the Gift from God /
        aka God's Gift
1986   Propos sur le cinéma / Reflections on the Cinema
1988   Zan Boko *[Moore]*
1991   Madame Hado

KABORÉ, Maurice Edmond   Burkina Faso

24.6.1955 Ouagadougou, Burkina Faso. After completing secondary school, he became an inspector for the National Institute of Statistics and Demography in Burkina Faso. Kaboré received his film training at the Institut Africain d'Education Cinématographique (INAFEC) in Ouagadougou. He worked as an assistant director on several films before directing his first film, the documentary *Emoro* in 1986.

Filmography

1986	Emoro
1987	Etre femme au Burkina / To Be a Woman in Burkina Faso

KAMBA, Sébastien   Congo

1941 Congo. He trained in France for two years. *La rançon d'une alliance / The Cost of an Alliance* (1973), made with assistance from the French Ministry of Co-operation, was the first Congolese feature film.

Filmography

1965	Le peuple du Congo-Léo vaincra / Victory to the Congolese People
1968	Apéa
	Le festival panafricain d'Alger / Panafrican Festival of Algiers
	Chine populaire sixième conférence / The People's Republic of China: the Sixth Conference
	Festival culturel de Guinée / Cultural Festival in Guinea
	La grande date / The Big Day
1973	La rançon d'une alliance / The Cost of an Alliance
1977	Le corps et l'esprit / Body and Spirit
	L'habitat en république populaire du Congo / The Environment in the People's Republic of the Congo
	Hommage au Président Marien Ngouabi / Homage to President Marien Ngouabi
1979	Tchi Kom Mbi

14.4.1943 Nkongsamba, western Cameroon. He attended primary school in Nkongsamba and secondary school in Douala. Kamwa then went to Paris to study economics but decided to take courses in film and dance at the Université de Paris VIII and at the Académie Internationale de Danse respectively. He also trained as a stage actor at the Actors Studio (1967-68). He acted in various stage plays, including Shakespeare's *The Merchant of Venice* and *Othello*. In 1972 he directed his first film *Boubou-cravate / Cross Breed* with financial assistance from the Consortium Audiovisuel International. He has formed his own production company, DK7 Films.

Filmography

1972	Boubou-cravate / Cross Breed
1975	Pousse-pousse / Tricycle Man / *aka* Rickshaw
1978	Chantal Rega
	La ligne de cœur / Line of the Heart
1979	Novotel
	Akum
	Danse automate, danse! / Dance, Automaton, Dance!
1980	Messe à Melen / Mass at Melen
	Notre fille / Our Daughter
1981	Cam-Air, dix ans d'essor / Cam Air, a Decade of Flight
1982	Nous les fous du volant / Such Crazy Driving
1983	Les fleurs du terroir / Flowers of the Soil
1987	La petite fille trouvée / Little Girl Found
1990	Video lire (5-part series)

KANTA, Abdou   Niger

1946 Foulatary, Niger. He studied at the Université de Paris where he graduated with a degree in literature as well as a diploma in cinema and television. Kanta is also a qualified French teacher. He has worked for Nigerian radio and television as a producer and has written several romantic books. He is also the president of the Association of Niger Film-Makers.

Filmography

1981	L'homme et les animaux / Man and the Animals
1982	Le divorce / The Divorce
	L'homme sans cicatrice / The Man Without a Scar
1990	Lelée

KAPLAN, Mark Jeremy   Zimbabwe

7.2.1953 Bulawayo, Zimbabwe. He grew up in South Africa. He studied at the University of Cape Town (grad. 1975) and at the Massachusetts Institute of Technology in Cambridge, MA (grad. 1985). Kaplan has been involved in video production and training work since 1979. Between 1980 and 1982 he was the first co-ordinator of the Community Video Resource Association (CVRA), based in the western Cape; it functioned primarily as a training facility serving a wide range of community-based organisations. As a result of his work Kaplan was held in solitary confinement for 53 days at the end of 1981 and deported from South Africa in August 1982. He co-founded the Capricorn Video Unit in Harare (1986), providing production and training facilities to the southern African region. He worked on various films as producer or co-producer, including *Biko: Breaking the Silence* (Edwina Spicer, 1988) and *Women in Theatre* (Capricorn Video Unit, 1990); he has also worked as a cameraman and editor. In 1989 he founded Intermedia which operates as a production arm of Capricorn Video Unit. His début film as a director is a documentary on the rise of worker co-operatives in Botswana and Zimbabwe and his most recent film is a video about maintenance law.

Filmography

1986	Bound to Strike Back (co-dir Richard Wicksteed)
1989	Only the Beginning
1990	Reconciliation in Zimbabwe: the First Ten Years
1991	Your Child Too

KHAN, Mohamed   Egypt

1942 Cairo, Egypt. Khan came to London to study film and also published a short English language book *An Introduction to the Egyptian Cinema* (1969). His prolific output and consistent quality have singled him out as one of the leading figures of the New Egyptian Realist group of directors.

Filmography

1980	Al-Th'ar / Vengeance
1981	Tair 'alal-tariq / Bird on the Road
1982	Maw'ad 'alal-'asha / Dinner Date
	Nesf arnab / Half a Million
1983	Al-Harrif / Streetplayer
1984	Kharaj wa lam ya'ud / Missing Person
1985	Mishwar 'Omar / Omar's Journey
1986	Youssef wa Zeinab / Youssef and Zeinab
	'Awdet muwatin / Return of a Citizen
1987	Zaugat ragul muhimm / Wife of an Important Man
1988	Ahlam Hind wa Camelia / Dreams of Hind and Camelia
1990	Supermarket
1991	Fares al-Medina / Knight of the City

See also: 11/IIb.

KHEMIR, Nacer   Tunisia

1948 Korba, Tunisia. He went to school in Khaznadard. Khemir is an accomplished self-taught sculptor, performing storyteller, writer and film-maker. His books include *Ogresse / Ogress* (1975) and *Schéhérazade* (1987).

Filmography

1984	Al-Ha'imoon / The Drifters
1990	Tawq al-Hamama al-Mafqud / The Lost Ring of the Dove
1991	A la recherche des 1001 nuits / Tales of 1001 Nights

KHLIFI, Omar

Tunisia

16.3.1934 Soliman, Tunisia. Khlifi is a self-taught film-maker who frequented cinema clubs and the Cinémathèque in Tunis during his youth. He is a founder member of the Association of Amateur Film-Makers. In 1959 he started his own production company and made his first amateur film, a short documentary on the history of Tunisia before independence.

Filmography

1965	Drame bédouin / Bedouin Drama
1966	Le défi / The Challenge
1972	Surakh / Screams

KONDE, Joseph

Burkina Faso

14.3.1952 Tougan, north-western Burkina Faso. After receiving his secondary education Konde enrolled at the Institut Africain d'Education Cinématographique (INAFEC) in Ouagadougou. After graduation he worked for national television in Burkina Faso. In 1984 he released his début film, the documentary *Préserver la santé au village / Protecting Health in the Village*.

Filmography

1984   Préserver la santé au village / Protecting Health in the Village

KOSSOKO, Yaya   Niger

1944 Sabalou, Benin. Kossoko studied film through a correspondence course. He worked with several film-makers including the Nigerian director **Ganda**. After working with Ganda on *Le wazzou polygame* (1970), Kossoko released his first film *La réussite de Mei Thebre / Mei Thebre's Success*. In 1977 he worked for Italian television on several short documentaries about life in Niger.

Filmography

1969	La réussite de Mei Thebre / Mei Thebre's Success
1978	Les hantés de la coqueluche
1981	La danse des génies / The Dance of the Spirits

KOULA, Jean-Louis   Ivory Coast

1950 Mona, Ivory Coast. He studied cinema at the Conservatoire Libre du Cinéma Français in Paris. He is a founder member of Les Films de la Montagne (1978). He worked as assistant to director **Fadika** during the shooting of *Djeli, conte d'aujourd'hui / Djeli, a Story of Today* (1981). He made his directorial début in 1979 with *Les masques guéré*.

Filmography

1979	Les masques guéré
1980	La Côte d'Ivoire et la mer / Ivory Coast and the Sea (co-dir **Kozoloa Yeo**)
	Adja Tio (A cause de l'héritage) / Adja Tio (Because of Inheritance)
	Textiles africains: des créateurs, pour quoi faire? / The Future for African Textile Design
	Les métiers du bâtiment / Building Crafts (co-dir **Kozoloa Yeo**)
1986	Carnaval de Bonoua / Bonoua Carnival
1987	Les petits métiers d'Abidjan / The Crafts of Abidjan

See also: 154/Ib, 154/If.

KOUMBA, Henri-Joseph   Gabon

1957 Omboué, Gabon. He studied cinema in Paris where he acquired most of his technical skills. He directed his first film in 1980.

Filmography

    1980   A l'aube du quatrième jour / At the Dawn of the Fourth Day
    1981   Vue générale du centre professionnel de N'Kembo / General View of the
                Professional Centre of N'Kembo
    1986   Le singe fou / The Mad Monkey

See also: 118b.

KOUYATE, Dany   Burkina Faso

1961 Bobo Dioulasso, Burkina Faso. He graduated from the Institut Africain d'Education Cinématographique (INAFEC) in Ouagadougou.

Filmography

    1989   Bilakoro [Dyula] (co-dir Falaba Issa Traoré, Sekou Traoré)
    1990   Tobbere kosam [Peul] / Poussière de lait / Milkdust (co-dir Philippe Baque)

See also: 141/IIf, 143/IIf.

KOUYATE, Djibril

1942 Bamako, Mali. After completing his early education in Bamako, he received a scholarship to study cinema in Moscow. Returning to Mali he worked in the film and video department of the Ministry of Information and made his directorial début in 1969. Kouyate is considered a pioneer of Malian cinema.

Filmography

1969	Arts et métiers / Arts and Crafts
1970	Le retour de Tiéman / The Return of Tiéman
1976	Le drapeau noir sur le berceau / The Black Flag on the Cradle
1978	Le Mali aujourd'hui / Mali Today

KTARI, Mohamed Nacer

Tunisia

17.5.1943 Sayada, Tunisia. After his secondary studies in Monastir, he went to Paris and enrolled at the Institut des Hautes Etudes Cinématographiques (IDHEC). He went on to Italy where he continued his film studies at the Istituto Luce in Rome. At the third congress of the Fédération Panafricaine des Cinéastes (FEPACI) in 1985 Ktari was elected northern regional secretary. He worked as an assistant director on many films, including Steven Spielberg's *Raiders of the Lost Ark* (1981). He made his first film in 1968.

Filmography

1968	Show 5000
1972	Prenons la ville / Let Us Take the Village
1973	Al-Safera / The Ambassadors
1983	L'autobus / Bus

KWAMI, Mambo N'Zinga   Zaïre

1943 Kinshasa, Zaïre. His original name was Roger Kwami which he changed after President Mobutu of Zaïre had introduced his policies of "authenticity" in 1971. He studied cinema at the Institut des Arts de Diffusion (IAD) in Louvain, Belgium. After graduation he worked for Belgian television. He has been president of the Zaïrean Organisation of Film-Makers (since 1983). He has made mostly documentaries.

Filmography

1972	Moseka
1974	Solidarité / Solidarity
1975	L'esprit de Salongo / The Spirit of Salongo
	Zamba-Zamba
1976	Festival national de la culture et des arts / National Festival of Culture and Arts
1977	Deuxième festival mondial des arts nègres-africains / Second World Festival of Black African Arts
1978	Premier congrès de l'UPRONA / First Congress of UPRONA
1980	Jean-Paul II au Zaïre / Jean-Paul II in Zaïre
1984	N'Gambo

LAHLOU, Latif   Morocco

1940 El Jadida, central Morocco. He studied film at the Institut des Hautes Etudes Cinématographiques (IDHEC) in Paris. After graduation he worked for a period as a director for French television. He returned to Tunisia where he continued working in television, this time with Moroccan television. In 1963 he directed his first film.

Filmography

1963	Cultivez la betterave / Grow Beetroot
1966	Fourrage / Fodder
1968	Du nouveau dans la vallée de Tassaout / Something New in the Valley of Tassaout
1970	Soleil de printemps / Spring Sunshine
1986	La compromission / The Compromise

LAHLOU, Nabyl   Morocco

1945 Fez, Morocco. For many years he wrote and produced several plays for the theatre. His directorial début in the cinema is a medium-length film which he also wrote and co-produced (1975).

Filmography

1975   The Dead
1978   El Kanfoudi
1980   Al-Hakem al-'am / The Governor General of Chakerbakerben Island
1984   Brahim Yach
       Nahr al-Roah / The Soul's River

LAKHDAR-HAMINA, Mohamed   Algeria

1934 M'Sila, northern Algeria. Lakhdar-Hamina is one of the leading figures in the Algerian cinema and for several years was head of the Algerian national film organisation.

Filmography

1966   Rih al-Awras / Le vent des Aurès / Wind of the Aurès
1968   Hassan Terro
1972   Décembre / December
1975   Waqai' sinin al-Jamr / La chronique des années de braise / Chronicle of
       the Years of Ashes
1982   Vent de sable / Sandstorm
1986   La dernière image / The Last Image

See also: 38/lb, 45/lb.

LALLEM, Ahmed   Algeria

10.8.1940 Algeria.   He studied cinema at the Institut des Hautes Etudes Cinématographiques (IDHEC) in Paris and at Poland's Łódź Film School. On his return to Algeria, he worked in television where he produced several documentaries.

Filmography

1966	Elles / The Women
	Auto construction
1967	Lauriers roses / Pink Laurels
	Le mouton / The Sheep
1968	Rencontres à Citra / Encounters at Citra
	Festival panafricain / Panafrican Festival
1969	Aujourd'hui, le hoggar / Today, the "Hoggar"
1971	Jeux universitaires Maghrebins / Maghreb University Games
1972	Al-Mantiqa al-Muharrama / Zone interdite / Forbidden Zone
1973	Politique forestière / Forestry Politics
1976	Barrière / Barrier
1977	Bab-ezzouar
	Solidarité / Solidarity
	Femmes de la céramique / Ceramics Craftswomen

LANCINE, Diaby   Ivory Coast

1956 Samatiguila, north-western Ivory Coast. He completed his secondary education and then studied cinema at the Conservatoire Libre du Cinéma Français in Paris.

Filmography

1987	La dernière heure de Sandra / Sandra's Last Hour
1988	L'amour blesse / Love Hurts
	Sanou
1990	L'africaine / The African

24.3.1943 Bordj Menaiel, Algeria. Laradji studied cinema at the Institut National du Cinéma in Algiers.

Filmography

1966	La poupée / The Doll
1969	La bombe / The Bomb
1970	Enfants du peuple / Children of the People
1972	Pour que vive l'Algérie / So That Algeria Lives
1973	SN SEMPAC
1974	Casbah 74
1975	El Djazair des Rais
1976	La Kalaa des Bani Hammad / The Citadel of Bani Hammad
	El Djazair al-Mahroussa / Algeria Protected
1977	Nassreddine Dinet
1978	Carthage
1979	Juba 11
1980	Djémila
1981	Massinissa
	Sakf wa 'aila / Un toit une famille / One Roof, One Family

LEVERI, Mark   Tanzania

1949 Dar es Salaam, Tanzania. He enrolled at the University of Dar es Salaam where he graduated with an honours degree in public administration and international relations. Leveri was a film trainee at the Audio Visual Institute, also in Dar es Salaam (1973-75). In 1975 he started working for the Tanzanian Film Company and is currently its general manager and executive producer.

Filmography *(all Swahili)*

1975	Chakula ni uhai / Food Is Life
1976	Nguo yako / Your Cloth
1978	Uvuvi / Fisheries
1980	Kilimo cha maksai / Farming With Oxen
	Mazingira na kipindupindu / Cholera and the Environment
1981	Shule ya kijamii / Community School
1982	Ufundi wa kujitegemea / Appropriate Technology

LLEDO, Jean-Pierre   Algeria

1947 Tlemcen, north-western Algeria. Lledo studied film at the VGIK film school in Moscow. He has written several articles in the now discontinued Algerian magazine *Al-Shashatan / Les deux écrans / The Two Screens* and made his directorial début in 1982.

Filmography

1982	Mamlakat al-Ahlam / Kingdom of Dreams
1990	Adhwa'a / Lights

LOUHICHI, Tayeb   Tunisia

June 1948 Mareth, Tunisia. He studied literature and has a doctorate in sociology. Louhichi studied cinematography at the Institut de Formation aux Métiers du Cinéma (IFCA) and at the Ecole Nationale Louis Lumière. He then made several short films. *Qariati bayna al-Qura / My Village Between the Villages* (1972) was awarded a Gold Tanit at the International Film Festival of Carthage in Tunis.

Filmography

1972   Qariati bayna al-Qura / My Village Between the Villages
1974   Ziara ou visite de / Ziara's Visit
1982   L'ombre de la terre / Shadow of the Earth

MABROUK, Nejia Ben   Tunisia

1949 El-Oudiane, Tunisia. She has dual Belgian/Tunisian nationality. Mabrouk studied French language and literature at university in Tunis (1969-71). She went to Brussels where she enrolled at the Institut National des Arts du Spectacle et Techniques de Diffusion (INSAS) (grad. 1976). Afterwards she worked as a trainee assistant for Belgian television before making her directorial début.

Filmography

1976   Pour vous servir / At Your Service
1978   Documentaire UNESCO / UNESCO Documentary
1982/8   La trace / The Trail
1991   The Search of Shaima

MAHOMO, Nana   South Africa

1930 Johannesburg, South Africa. He was born into the Suto ethnic group whose family came from Lesotho. He grew up in Soweto where he attended both primary and secondary school. Mahomo then left for Cape Town where he enrolled at the university to study law. During this period Mahomo joined the Pan-Africanist Congress (PAC) and was asked by its president to represent the organisation abroad. Mahomo arrived in England (1960) and travelled extensively in Europe, delivering lectures. He increasingly felt the desire and need to make films to counteract the pro-apartheid propaganda films produced by the South African Information Service. Without any formal training in film-making, Mahomo and a group of other South Africans in exile formed Morena Films, a London-based production company. It was through this company that he made his first film *Phela Ndaba / End of Dialogue* (1969).

Filmography

1969   Phela Ndaba / End of Dialogue
1974   Last Grave at Dimbaza

MAIGA, Djingareye   Niger

1939 Ouatagouna, Mali. He is a self-taught film-maker and has also worked as an actor.

Filmography

1972   Le ballon / The Ball
1975   L'étoile noire / The Black Star
1979   Autour de l'hippopotame / Round the Hippopotamus (co-dir Yves Billon)
        Nuages noirs / Black Clouds
1980   Ouatagouna (co-dir Yves Billon, Jean-François Schiano)
1981   Les rendez-vous du 15 avril / Meetings on the 15th of April
1982   La danse des dieux / Dance of the Gods
1983   Aube noire / Black Dawn
1984   Intronisation / Enthronement
        Paysans des sables / Peasants of the Sands
1987   Paysans du fleuve / Peasants of the River

MAREDZA, Claude   Zimbabwe

22.12.1958 Norumedzo village, southern Zimbabwe. After completing his primary education at schools in Norumedzo and Chikuku, Maredza went to Silveira School, part of a catholic mission and completed his secondary schooling. In 1978 he enrolled at the University of Zimbabwe to study accountancy (grad. 1983). He worked briefly for a firm of chartered accountants in Harare and for various other companies. Maredza has acted in the theatre and appeared in various television plays; he was also the main actor in the 1983 film *The House of Hunger*, directed by Chris Austin and based on a novel by Dambudzo Marechera.

Filmography

1982   Harurwa

MARUMA, Olley Tsino   Zimbabwe

1.5.1953 Bulawayo, south-western Zimbabwe. Maruma studied law at the University of Kent at Canterbury in England. He took a vocational training course in television production (September 1978-April 1979) supported by the British Council and the BBC. In 1983 he joined Vacari Films and completed a course in film-making at the Société Française de Production Cinématographique (SFPC). Maruma has worked as a producer-director of weekly television and radio programmes for the Zimbabwe Broadcasting Corporation. He also worked as scriptwriter and executive producer on the Zimbabwean film *Biko: Breaking the Silence* (Edwina Spicer, 1988).

Filmography

1981   Quest for Freedom
1982   The Assegaï
1986   After the Hunger and Drought
1987   Consequences

MARZUQ, Sa'id   Egypt

26.10.1940 Cairo, Egypt. He studied film whilst working at Studio Misr (from 1955) and also was a painter and sculptor. Marzuq then worked as an assistant director and (from 1964) as a director for television. He made several short films before directing features for the cinema (1971).

Filmography

1966	Onchoudet al-Salam / The Song of Peace
1968	Adaa' al-Haya / The Enemies of Life
1969	Toboul / Drums
1970	Demoue al-Salam / The Tears of Peace
1971	Zawgati wal kalb / My Wife and the Dog
1972	Al-Khawf / The Fear
1974	Aridu hallan / I Want an Answer
1975	Al-Modhniboon / The Guilty
1985	Inqadh ma yumkin inqadhuhu / Save What We Can
1988	Ayyam al-Ru'b / Days of Terror
1989	Al-Mughtasibun / The Rapists

MASOKOANE, Glen Ujebe   South Africa

11.12.1950 Johannesburg, South Africa. His interest in cinema began at the age of eight. He would project images on a wall through a magnifying glass using a candle as a light source and this created illusions of movement. In 1970 he enrolled to study political science at the University of Fort Hare in the eastern Cape; he was expelled for political reasons (1972). In the same year he founded the People's Experimental Theatre (PET), a radical black consciousness theatre. He left South Africa in January 1973 and went to Nigeria where he studied mass communication at the University of Lagos (grad. 1978). After graduation he enrolled at the London International Film School where he graduated with a diploma in the technique of film production and direction. In 1984 he joined the London-based Ceddo Film and Video Workshop where he worked as a producer/director and also organised film and video training courses for black youths in the United Kingdom. He was the producer of the UK film *Time and Judgment* (Menelik Shabazz, 1988).

Filmography

1984   The Suit
1987   We Are the Elephant
1989   Beyond the Culture of Silence (unreleased)

MAZIF, Sid Ali   Algeria

16.10.1943 Algiers. He studied cinema at the Institut National du Cinéma.

Filmography

1966	Trois soldats Essai
	La vie à deux / Living Together
1968	Cueillette des oranges / Orange Picking
	Le paludisme / Malaria
	La rencontre, à l'enfer à dix ans / Hell At the Age of Ten
1969	Sucreries d'El Khemis / Sweet Making in El Khemis
	Le messager / The Messenger
1971	Nifta
	Sueur noire / Black Sweat
1972	Les étudiants dans la campagne / Students in the Countryside
1975	Masirat al-Ru'ah / Les nomades / The Nomads
1978	Leila et les autres / Leila and the Others
1982	J'existe / I Exist

See also: 45/Ib.

M'BAYE, Ousmane William   Senegal

31.8.1952 Paris, France. M'Baye trained at the Conservatoire Libre du Cinéma Français.
He continued his studies at the Université de Paris VII. His first film is a short - *Doomi
Ngacc / L'enfant de Ngatch / Ngatch's Child* (1979).

Filmography

1979	Doomi Ngacc *[Wolof]* / L'enfant de Ngatch / Ngatch's Child
1983	Dunde Yakaar / Pain sec / Dry Bread
1989	Dakar Clando (*ep.* in *City Life* omnibus film)

MBUGU-SCHELLING, Flora   Tanzania

1959 Moshi near Mount Kilimanjaro, northern Tanzania.   Mbugu-Schelling studied journalism at the Tanzanian School of Journalism. In 1985 she completed a four-year audio visual course at the Adolf Lazi Schule in Esslingen near Stuttgart in Germany.

Filmography

1986   Kumekucha *[Swahili]* / The Dawn

MEDA, Bemile Stanilas   Burkina Faso

15.5.1958 Burkina Faso.   Meda studied cinema at the Institut Africain d'Education Cinématographique (INAFEC) in Ouagadougou. He has a degree in science and audio visual techniques and a masters certificate in English from the Université de Ouagadougou. He was at one time director of the National Board of Film Production in Burkina Faso.

Filmography

1984   L'eau, fruit du travail / The Fruit of One's Labour
1989   Koligure / La gardienne des champs / The Guardian of the Fields

MEDEIROS, Richard Beby de   Benin

1940 Ouidah, southern Benin. He received his early education in Ouidah. After secondary school he registered at the Université Nationale du Bénin in Cotonou where he studied literature. Medeiros taught at the university for a period before going to France to continue his studies. During his stay there he came into contact with the cinema. In 1970 he produced and directed a short film *Le roi est mort en exil / The King Has Died in Exile* for Algerian television.

Filmography

1970	Le roi est mort en exil / The King Has Died in Exile
1972	Téké, hymne au Borgou / Téké, Hymn to Borgou
	Silence et feu de brousse / Silence and Bush Fire
1977	Le nouveau venu / The Newly Arrived

MENSAH, Charles   Gabon

1948 Libreville, Gabon. He received his training in film at the National Film and Television School in Gabon. After graduation he worked for Gabonese television. Since 1985 he has been assistant general manager of the Gabonese National Film Institute (CENACI).

Filmography

1973	La grasse matinée / Lazy Morning
1975	Les trois de cœur / The Three of Hearts
1976	Obali (co-dir **Pierre-Marie Dong**)
1977	Ayouma (co-dir **Pierre-Marie Dong**)
1978	Ilombé (co-dir Christian Gavarry)
1983	L'érable et l'okoumé / The Maple and the Gaboon (co-dir Pierre Castonguay)

See also: 59/lf, 118/lb.

MERBAH, Mohamed Lamine   Algeria

28.7.1946 Tighennif, Algeria. Merbah studied cinema at the Institut National du Cinéma and sociology at the Université d'Alger. After graduation he directed many documentaries for Algerian television.

Filmography

1969	El Montasser / The Winner
1971	Yades
	La mission / The Mission
1972	Les médailles / The Medals
	Les spoliateurs / The Despoilers
	Belkacem el Bourgeoisi
1974	Chaabia
1975	Les révoltes / The Revolts
1976	Beni hendel / The Uprooted

MHANDO, Martin   Tanzania

7.6.1952 Mbulu, northern Tanzania. In 1973 he enrolled at the University of Dar es Salaam (grad. 1976). In the same year he took a short course at the Tanzanian School of Journalism and was immediately offered a job as a journalist for the Ministry of Information. He travelled to Romania (1977) where he took a postgraduate course in film at the Institute of Theatre and Film Art in Bucharest. On his return Mhando joined the Tanzanian Film Company where he now occasionally works.

Filmography

1979	The Underground Voice
1981	Bishop Kiwovele
1982	Challenge Cup
	Super League, Super Champions
1985	Yomba Yomba
1986	África na Suécia / Africa in Sweden (co-dir **Luis Manuel Martino Simão**)
1987	Mama tumaini *[Swahili]* / Women of Hope (co-dir Sigue Endresen)
1990	SADCC: the First Decade

See also: 130/lf.

MINOT, Gilbert Claude   Guinea

1937 Paris, France. He studied cinema in Los Angeles. His filmography to date consists entirely of commentaries on political or cultural subjects. In 1969 he travelled to Algeria where he made a documentary on the Algiers Panafrican Cultural Festival (1970).

Filmography

1970	Le festival panafricain d'Alger / Algiers Panafrican Cultural Festival
1971	Le 22 novembre / 22 November
1973	L'homme et l'environnement / Man and the Environment

MORY, Philippe   Gabon

1932 Batanga, Gabon. He studied cinema in France and has acted in several films, including *On n'enterre pas le dimanche / We Don't Bury On Sundays* (Michel Drach, 1959). He also worked as an assistant to Drach and wrote the script for and acted in *La cage / The Cage* (Robert Darène, 1962). Mory was general manager of the Gabonese National Film Institute (CENACI) in Libreville (1975-85). He has directed and produced several commercials for the national airline Air Gabon and for the Ministry of Tourism.

Filmography

1972	Les tam tams se sont tus / The Tam-Tams Are Silent
1977	Oua
1978	Un enfant du village / Child of the Village
1980	Dix ans de rénovation / Ten Years of Renovation

MOUKETA, Paul   Gabon

1958 Mouila, south-western Gabon. After secondary school he pursued his studies in Saint-Cloud, Paris. Mouketa also holds a diploma in anthropology from the Université de Nanterre.

Filmography

1983	Anthropologie visuelle / Visual Anthropology
1984	Regards au pluriel / Different Points of View
1985	Dominique Douma
	Le vétéran / The Veteran
1986	Raphia / Raffia

MWEZE, N'Gangura   Zaïre

1950 Bukavu, Kivu region, eastern Zaïre. After secondary school he went to Louvain in Belgium where he studied at the Institut des Arts de Diffusion (IAD) (grad. 1976). Returning to Zaïre, Mweze became a teacher in film at the Institut National des Arts (INA) in Kinshasa. He was also offered a job as the chief of the audio visual section at the Musée National in Zaïre. He is a member of the National Organisation of Film Producers of Zaïre and the International Council of Film and Television Zaïre.

Filmography

1973	Tam-tam électronique / Electronic Tam-Tam
1975	Rhythm and Blood
1980	Chéri Samba, peintre / Chéri Samba, Painter
1984	Kin Kiesse
1987	La vie est belle / Life Is Beautiful (co-dir Benoît Lamy)

NASRALLAH, Yousry   Egypt

26.7.1952 Cairo, Egypt. At the age of seven he saw his first film, the American *Journey to the Center of the Earth* (Henry Levin, 1959). Nasrallah knew from that moment that he wanted to work in the cinema. After studying economics and mathematics at Cairo University he participated in the movement against Nasser's one-party system. He also spent four years in West Beirut writing about cinema for the Libyan newspaper *As-Safir*. He worked on films directed by the Syrian Omar Amiralay, Egyptian **Chahine** and German Volker Schlöndorff. Chahine produced Nasrallah's directorial début *Sarikat sayfeya / Summersaults* (1988) from a script which Nasrallah had begun writing in 1985.

Filmography

1988   Sarikat sayfeya / Summersaults

N'DABIAN, Vodio Etienne   Ivory Coast

1938 Grand Lahou, Ivory Coast; died 1987. He attended primary school in the Ivory Coast and completed his secondary schooling and further education in France. He studied cinema at VGIK in Moscow and finished his training in Rome. He has worked for national television in the Ivory Coast (since 1967).

Filmography

1967   Energie électrique / Electric Energy
1972   Le cri du muezzin / The Cry of the Muezzin
1975   Les collégiennes / The Schoolgirls

1945 Dakar, Senegal. He completed his primary and secondary education in Dakar and then studied film at the Université de Paris VIII. His output consists almost entirely of documentaries.

Filmography

1975	Perantal
1976	La confrérie des Mourides / The Mourides Brotherhood
	L'exode rural au Sénégal / Rural Depopulation in Senegal
1978	Pêcheurs de Kayar / The Fishers of Stones
	Problèmes de l'espace et du logement en France / Space and Housing Problems in France
1979	Geti Tey *[Wolof]* / La pêche aujourd'hui / Fishing Today
	Les Halles, l'ancien marché / The Old Covered Market
1986	La santé une aventure peu ordinaire / Remarkable Efforts in Health Care
1989	Aqua
	Chaudronnerie d'art / The Craft of the Metal Worker
	Les chutes de Ngalam / The Ngalam Falls
	Les malles / The Trunks
1990	Diplomate à la tomate / Diplomat My Foot

NEE-OWOO, Kwate   Ghana

1944 Ghana. Nee-Owoo came to London to study at the London International Film School where he graduated with a degree in film technique (1969). His début film was made in London (1972). In 1977 he was offered the post of head of the Media Research Unit at the Institute of African Studies at the University of Ghana. Nee-Owoo is a member of the Fédération Panafricaine des Cinéastes (FEPACI) and also of the Philadelphia Film-Makers Workshop in the United States. He has served as a jury member at the International Film Festival of Carthage in Tunis and at the Ouagadougou International Film Festival in Burkina Faso.

Filmography

1972	You Hide Me
1980	Gold - The Traditional Lost Wax Process
1984	Okyeame Akuffo - State Linguist
1988	Ouaga: African Cinema Now! (co-dir Kwesi Owusu)
1991	Ama

NGAKANE, Lionel   South Africa

1928 Pretoria, South Africa. He studied at the University of the Witwatersrand in Johannesburg. After a short spell as a journalist Ngakane began his career as an actor, including a part in the British film *Cry the Beloved Country* (Zoltan Korda, 1951) as well as many television and theatre productions. He is a founder member of the Fédération Panafricaine des Cinéastes (FEPACI) and participates in many symposia and colloquia on African and third world cinema. His first film as a director was a documentary on South Africa; his feature début *Jemima and Johnny* (1966) received several major festival awards.

Filmography

1964	Bantou debout! / Vukani Awake!
1966	Jemima and Johnny
1975	Once Upon a Time
1985	Nelson Mandela
1988	Canariv
1989	Nigerian Transit

NGASSA, Jean-Paul   Cameroon

1939 Bafang, Cameroon.   He studied cinema at the Ecole Supérieure d'Etudes Cinématographiques (ESEC) in Paris. In 1962 he co-directed his first medium-length film *Aventure en France / Adventure in France*.

Filmography

1962	Aventure en France / Adventure in France (co-dir Philippe Brunet)
1965	La grande case Bamiléké / The Large Bamiléké Hut (co-dir William Hamon)
1970	Une nation est née / A Nation Is Born

N'GOUNOU, Michel   Cameroon

Cameroon. N'Gounou studied cinema in Paris, France. During his stay in Paris he worked as a fashion model to supplement his small income.

Filmography

| 1981 | L'adoption et le divorce / Adoption and Divorce |
| 1983 | Trait d'union / Mixed Features |

NIKIEMA, Boureima

Burkina Faso

1941 Ouahigouya, northern Burkina Faso. He studied at the Centre d'Etudes des Sciences et Techniques de l'Information at the Université Cheikh Anta Diop de Dakar in Senegal; he also studied film in West Germany. Nikiema trained and worked as a journalist for a period before making his début as a film director (1988).

Filmography

1988	Foyer amelioré / Home Improvement
1989	Ma fille ne sera pas excisée / My Daughter Will Not Be Circumcised
1990	Dynamique de la réhabilitation de l'environnement / Dynamics of Environmental Rehabilitation
1991	Saya II
	Trait d'union / The Link

OGUNDE, Chief Hubert

Nigeria

10.7.1916 Ososa, Nigeria; died 4.4.1990 London. His father was a Baptist minister. He attended schools in Ososa, Lagos and Ijebu-Ode and became a teacher and organist (1933). After schooling Ogunde worked in the police force for several years (1941-46). In this period he acted and wrote plays: the first to be performed was the religious-based opera *The Garden of Eden and The Throne of God* (1944). In 1946 he left the police force and founded the first professional theatre company in Nigeria, the African Music Research Company. Ogunde was opposed to British colonialism and his politically subversive productions, including *Worse Than Crime, Tiger's Empire, Strike and Hunger* and particularly *Yoruba ronu / Yorubas, Think!* (1964), were banned for many years. As a result of his efforts to stage plays, he was often arrested and fined. He was commissioned by prime minister Abubakar Tafawa Balewa to produce the play *Song of Unity* to commemorate the full independence of Nigeria (1960). Ogunde was a leading figure in the Yoruba folk travelling theatre tradition and is acknowledged as the father of modern Nigerian theatre. His extensive writing and performing career comprised over fifty plays for the theatre and he served as actor-manager, choreographer, dancer, composer and musician of his theatrical company. Fellow Nigerian film-maker **Balogun** made a film adaptation of Ogunde's play *Aîye* in 1979 and two years later Ogunde made his own directorial début in the cinema; all his films are adaptations of his own plays. He also appeared in the American film set in Nigeria, *Mister Johnson* (Bruce Beresford, 1990).

Filmography *[all Yoruba]*

1981	Jaiyesimi (co-dir Freddie Goode)
1982	Aropin N'Tenia (co-dir Freddie Goode)
1986	Ayanmo / Destiny

OKIOH, François Sourou   Benin

1950 Lema, Nigeria. He received his primary and secondary school in Lema. Okioh studied modern literature and history at university before joining the faculty of film and television at FAMU in Prague. He has written several books on poetry. He directed his first film *Ces collines ne sont pas muettes / These Hills Are Not Mute* in 1980.

Filmography

1980	Ces collines ne sont pas muettes / These Hills Are Not Mute
1982	Odo te gban lo / Le fleuve a tout emporté / The Flood Has Swept Everything Away
	Me voici / Here I Am
1983	Ogu
1985	Ironu / Méditations / Meditations
1986	Enfants de... / Children of...
1991	Les tresseurs de corde / The Rope Plaiters

OLIVEIRA, Carlos Mendes de   Mozambique

8.4.1947 Porto, Portugal. In 1962 he emigrated to Mozambique with his family. He dropped out of a medical course and worked as a journalist (1970-1981). Oliveira then worked as a radio reporter and as a correspondent for the magazine *Tempo* and the daily newspaper *Notícias*. In 1981 he was offered the post of head of children's cinema at the Instituto Nacional de Cinema (INC), Mozambique's national film institute in Maputo; he was also head of department for arts and animation. He has written a book on Mozambican theatre *Pesquisas para um teatro popular em Moçambique / Research For a Popular Theatre in Mozambique*.

Filmography

1981	Jogos e brincadeiras / Fun and Games (co-dir Anna Fresu)
	Contos do coelho / Tales of the Rabbit
1982	O fogo / The Fire (co-dir Anna Fresu)
1983	Nós crianças Moçambicanas / We, Mozambican Children
	Aventuras do jovem taca / The Adventures of Young Taca
1984	Na estrada / On the Road
	A lua e a filma que não sabia pilar

OUEDRAOGO, Hamadou   Burkina Faso

1946 Yatenga province, northern Burkina Faso. After secondary school he went to France where he worked at a variety of jobs, including one as a journalist. He has been involved with several films and in 1978 made a short documentary *Yiki-Yan / Debout! / Get Up!* which received the Jury's Special Prize at the 6th Festival Panafricain du Cinéma de Ouagadougou (FESPACO) in 1979.

Filmography

1978	Yiki-Yan / Debout! / Get Up!
1981	L'exil / Exile
1983	Le Yatenga hier et aujourd'hui / Yatenga Yesterday and Today
1985	Larmes d'un enfant / A Child's Tears

OUEDRAOGO, Idrissa   Burkina Faso

21.1.1954 Banfora, south-western Burkina Faso. His parents are farmers. He started his primary education at a local school and was then sent to the capital Ouagadougou to continue his studies. When he was at secondary school Ouedraogo would save a few coins every weekend to go to the movies. After his schooling he went to the Institut Africain d'Education Cinématographique (INAFEC) in Ouagadougou to study film-making - he claims that he did not want to be a teacher and that the film institute was near his house. After his film studies Ouedraogo worked as a civil servant in film production management and produced his first short film *Poko* (1981), followed by several others (1983-85). After a short period in Kiev in the Ukraine, he enrolled at the Institut des Hautes Etudes Cinématographiques (IDHEC) in Paris (grad. 1985). In his first feature-length film *Yam daabo / Le choix / The Choice* (1986) he depicts a family struggling to be independent during drought and famine. The themes of rural life recur in his next films *Yaaba* (1989) and *Tilaï* (1990), which were both widely screened and acclaimed.

Filmography

1981	Poko *[Moore]*
1983	Les écuelles / The Platters / *aka* The Bowls
	Les funérailles du Larle Naba / Larle Naba's Funeral / *aka* The Funeral of Larle Naba (co-dir Pierre Rovamba)
1985	Ouagadougou, Ouaga deux roues / Ouagadougou, Ouaga Two Wheels
	Issa le tisserand / Issa the Weaver
	Tenga *[Moore]*
1986	Yam daabo *[Moore]* / Le choix / The Choice
1989	Yaaba *[Moore]* / Grandmother
1990	Tilaï *[Moore]* / Question d'honneur / A Question of Honour
1991	A Karim Na Sala / Karim et Sala / Karim and Sala

See also: 152b.

OUEDRAOGO, Sekou   Burkina Faso

23.2.1937 Fada N'Gourma, western Burkina Faso. Ouedraogo is considered one of the pioneers of cinema in Burkina Faso. He made several short films for television and for the community development programmme.

Filmography

1969   Foires générales voltaïques / The Great Fairs of Upper Volta

OUSSEINI, Inoussa   Niger

9.9.1950 Kellé, Niger. He gave up his secondary education a year early to become an assistant to the French film-maker Serge Moati who had been making films in Niger. Ousseini started a film club in Niamey and also contributed to the setting up of a journal *Synthèse nigérienne*, where he wrote many articles on the cinema. He went to France to study sociology at the Université de Tours. Between 1979 and 1984 he was secretary general of the Consortium Interafricain de Distribution Cinématographique (CIDC), the panafrican consortium of film distribution and production.

Filmography

1970   La sangsue / The Leech
1974   Paris, c'est joli / Paris Is Fun
1975   Ganga (co-dir Jean Rouch)
1976   Médecines et médecins / Doctors and Their Medicine (co-dir Jean Rouch)
1977   Une jeunesse face à la culture / A Youth in the Face of Culture
        Lutte saharienne / Saharan Struggle
1979   Wasan Kara
1980   Fêtes et traditions populaires du Niger / Popular Celebrations and
            Traditions of Niger
        Le soro
        Fantasia
1986   Taoua an 2 le festival / Taoua Year 2 the Festival

OYEKUNLE, Olusegun   Nigeria

1944 Egbe, south-western Nigeria. After completing his secondary schooling in Zaria, he trained in film studies in Los Angeles. He has worked in the theatre and written several plays.

Filmography

1980	Ugun Abade
1982	Parcel Post

PROCTOR, Elaine   South Africa

10.7.1960 Johannesburg, South Africa. She spent much of her youth in rural Africa. Proctor worked as an actress with the Market Theater of Johannesburg and was involved in community film projects. She studied at the London International Film School (1982) and then founded Loy Films, an independent production company which also trained young black technicians (1983). In 1986 she registered at the National Film and Television School at Beaconsfield in England. Between 1983 and 1986 she directed documentaries; her début full-length feature film *On the Wire* (1990) is an exploration of apartheid.

Filmography

1983	Eyes To See To Read
1984	Re Tla Bona *[Northern Sotho]* / We Will See
1986	Sharpeville Spirit
1988	Palesa
1990	On the Wire
1992	Friends

RACHEDI, Ahmed   Algeria

1938 Tebessa, north-eastern Algeria. He worked with the French director René Vautier during the war of liberation. After independence (1962) Rachedi, together with Vautier and others, became director of the Audio Visual Centre in Algiers. In 1967 he was appointed head of the Office National pour le Commerce et l'Industrie Cinématographique (ONCIC), Algeria's film bureau, a position he held until 1974. He has since formed his own audio visual company.

Filmography

1962	Referendum
1963	People on the Move
1964	Problems of Youth
	Hands Like Birds
	Cuba Yes
	The Ouadhias
1965	Fajr al-Mu'adhdhabin / L'aube des damnés / The Dawn of the Damned
1966	The Commune
1967	Election
1969	Al-Afyun wal-'asa / L'opium et le bâton / Fighting Opium / aka The Opium and the Stick
1972	Why Does Algeria Live?
1973	Le doigt dans l'engrenage / The Law in the System
1980	Ali fi bilad al-Sarab / Ali aux pays des mirages / Ali in Wonderland
1981	Es Silene
1982	Tahunat al-Sayyid Fabré / Le moulin de M. Fabré / Mr Fabré's Mill

See also: 45/Ib.

RAEBURN, Michael   Zimbabwe

1943 Cairo, Egypt. From the age of three he lived in Rhodesia (now Zimbabwe) and studied at St George's College in Salisbury and the University College of Rhodesia and Nyasaland (grad. 1965). He then continued his studies at the University of London. He studied film at the Université d'Aix-Marseille and at the Institut des Hautes Etudes Cinématographiques (IDHEC) in Paris. In 1968 he made his first film, the political documentary *Rhodesia Countdown* which caused trouble with the Rhodesian authorities. Consequently Raeburn was forced to leave the country and continued to make films in exile (1968-80). He has written a book about the war in Zimbabwe *Black Fire!* (1978) and served as producer on the UK film *Requiem for a Village* (David Gladwell, 1975).

Filmography

1968	Rhodesia Countdown
1971	The Plastic Shamrock
1974	This Is Renée
	It's In My Blood
	This Game of Golf
1976	Beyond the Plains Where Man Was Born
1979	Sunday Sweet Sunday
1984	The Grass Is Singing / *aka* Killing Heat
1988	Under African Skies (TV series)
1990	Jit
1991	Soweto

RAJAONARIVELO, Raymond   Madagascar

7.3.1949 Antananarivo, Madagascar. He received his primary and secondary education in Antananarivo. In 1972 he enrolled at the Université de Montpellier III (Université Paul Valéry) in France where he studied cinema. After graduating (1975) he continued his studies in cinema at the Université de Paris.

Filmography

1974	Izao lokanga ilao valiha *[Malagasy]*
1978	Babay sa lovohitra *[Malagasy]*
1988	Tabataba *[Malagasy]*

RAMAKA, Joseph Gai   Senegal

November 1952 St Louis, Senegal. He received his primary and secondary education in Senegal and then studied cinema at the Institut Polytechnique des Arts Cinématographiques in Paris. He worked as an assistant director, editor and director of photography on several African films. In 1985 he made his first film *Baw Naan*.

Filmography

1985	Baw Naan
1986	La musique lyrique peul / Lyrical Music of the Peul
	Portrait d'une mannequin / Portrait of a Model
1989	Nitt... n'doxx *[Wolof]* / Les faiseurs de pluie / Rain-Makers

RAMAMPY, Benoît Maurice   Madagascar

21.3.1947 Ambalavao, Madagascar. He completed his film training as a cameraman at OCORA/Radio France in Paris. On his return to Madagascar he enrolled at the Malagasy Production Centre where he furthered his studies in film production and directed several educational films.

Filmography

1972	L'accident / The Accident
1983	Le barrage de Namorona / The Namorona Dam
1984	Dahalo, dahalo
1987	Le prix de la paix / The Price of Peace (co-dir Abel Rakotozanamy)

RANDRASANA, Ignace-Solo   Madagascar

Madagascar. After completing his schooling, Randrasana worked for the Ministry of the Environment in Madagascar before joining the Malagasy Production Centre where he worked as an assistant director. At the same time he took a course in film-making.

Filmography

1973   Very remby *[Malagasy]* / Le retour / The Return
1987   Ilo tsy very *[Malagasy]* / Mad 47

REGGAB, Mohamed   Morocco

1942 Safi, Morocco. Reggab studied film at VGIK, the film school in Moscow. Returning to Morocco, he worked with **Derkaoui** and other colleagues on a jointly made film (1979).

Filmography

1979   Les cendres du clos / The Cinders of the Yard (co-dir **Mustapha Abdelkrim Derkaoui**)
1982   Hallaq darb al-Foqara / The Barber of the Poor Quarter

See also: 51/IIb, 51/IIf.

He has worked primarily for television, but his three most recent films are features for the cinema. His work is often concerned with the themes of nationalism and fascism, inter-racial relationships, apartheid and the social position of the Afrikaner. Working both in English and Afrikaans, he has directed films in many genres, including melodrama, comedy, musical and television series. Van Rensburg has acted as producer on the films *Crazy People* (1977), *City Lovers* (1981) and *Country Lovers* (1982). He is also a founder member of the Film and Allied Workers Union (FAWU), a radical South African film organisation.

Filmography

1971	Freddie's in Love
1973	Die bankrower / The Bank Robber
1974	Geluksdal / Happy Valley
1975	Willem (TV series)
	Die square / The Square (TV series)
1976	Oom Willem en die lord / Uncle Willem and the Lord
1979	Mickey Kannis Caught My Eye
1980	Good News (TV series)
	Die avonture van Joachim Verwey / The Adventures of Joachim Verwey (TV series)
1981	Doktor Con Viljee se Overberg / The Overberg of Doctor Con Viljee
1982	Anna Meintjies
	Sagmoedige neelsie / Gentle Johnny (TV series)
	Verspeelde lente / Lost Springtime (TV series)
	Die perdesmous / The Horse Trader
1984	Die vuurtoring / The Lighthouse
1985	Heroes (TV series)
1986	The Mantis Project (TV series)
1989	The Fourth Reich
	The Native Who Caused All the Trouble
1990	Taxi to Soweto

See also: 37/IIb.

RÉVIGNÉ, Georges-Gauthier   Gabon

1950 Douala, Cameroon. He studied at the Institut des Arts de Diffusion (IAD) in Louvain, Belgium. He worked as an assistant to directors **Dong** and **Mensah** on their co-directed film *Ayouma* (1977) and appeared as an actor in the film *Le singe fou / The Mad Monkey* (**Koumba**, 1986).

Filmography

1974	Maroga, une première / Maroga, a First
1979	Si Port Gentil m'était conté / The Story of Port Gentil
1980	La COMILOG
1981	Un homme, une visite-rencontre avec Gilles Saua / A Man, an Encounter with Gilles Saua
	Du Cap Lopez à Port Gentil / From Cap Lopez to Port Gentil
1983	Un cri dans la nuit / A Cry in the Night (uncompleted)

RIBEIRO, Thomas F   Ghana

2.2.1935 Ghana. Ribeiro studied in the United States and is a graduate of the City University of New York and the Radio Corporation of America (RCA). After graduation (1965) he worked as an assistant director for the Jack Glean Incorporation, producers of feature films and television commercials. He has written many scripts and directed numerous documentaries and several feature films. He was also assistant director on the American musical documentary *Soul to Soul* (Denis Sanders, 1971).

Filmography

1977	Genesis Chapter X
1983	The Visitor

1962 Johannesburg, South Africa. He enrolled at the University of the Witwatersrand in Johannesburg intending to study drama, but left after just one week to work in films. He entered the film industry as assistant director on the South African films *Two Weeks in Paradise* (Gray Hofmeyr, 1984) and *You Must Be Joking* (Elmo de Witt, 1986) but also began directing his own films in this period. His first films were made in collaboration with producer Anant Singh. The anti-apartheid *Place of Weeping* (1986) and the anti-war *The Stick* (1987) were both widely screened at international festivals and won many prizes and awards; after struggles with the censor the latter film was released in South Africa in 1991. Roodt was given the Standard Bank Award for best young film-maker in his country (1991). He usually writes the scripts for his films.

Filmography

1983	Mr TNT
1985	Wind Rider
1986	City of Blood
	Place of Weeping
1987	Tenth of a Second
	The Stick
1989	Jobman
1990	Cry the Beloved Country
	Geliefde land / Beloved Country
	American Kickboxer II
1991	Lightning Bird
	To the Death
	Chain of Desire
1992	Sarafina

27.10.1926 Alexandria, Egypt. His father was a doctor and a high-ranking civil servant. Saleh completed his secondary studies at Victoria College in Alexandria and obtained a degree in English literature (1949). Passionate about Shakespeare, Saleh ran the School of Literature's theatre group at Cairo University (1948-49). He worked as an assistant to **Chahine** (1954) before making his own directorial début a year later. He has also produced several short or medium-length films (1959-60; 1976) and is widely regarded as a pioneer of contemporary Egyptian cinema.

Filmography

1955	Darb al-Mahabil / Alley of Fools
1959	Al-'ara'is / The Marionettes
1960	Man nahnu / Who Are We?
	Nahwa al-Majhul / Towards the Unknown
1961	Siret al-Abtal / Struggle of the Heroes
1966	Al-Mutamarridoon / The Rebels
1968	Yawmiyyat na'ib fil-aryaf / Diary of the Village Investigator
1969	Al-Sayed al-Bolti
1972	Al-Makhdu'un / The Deceived
1976	Fajr al-Hadara: al-Fann al-Summari / The Dawn of Civilisation: the Art of Sumer
1981	Al-Ayyam al-Tawila / Long Days

See also: 36/lb.

SAMB-MAKHARAM, Ababacar   Senegal

21.10.1934 Dakar, Senegal; died September 1987. He was a Muslim of Lebou origin; his parents and family were farmers and fishermen. He left school and started working in various odd jobs. In 1953 he managed to finance his trip to Paris where he studied electrical engineering (1953-55). He later received a French government scholarship to study drama at the Centre d'Art Dramatique de la rue Blanche (1956). Samb-Makharam became a member of a black theatre group which performed plays by black and African writers. He also acted in various productions including several films. He then studied film-making at the Centro Sperimentale di Cinematografia in Rome (1959-62). He returned to Senegal (1964) and worked at the Ministry of Information before joining the Senegalese News Programme as a cameraman. Samb-Makharam made one short film (1965) before completing two features about African cultural life. In 1971 he was appointed secretary general of the Fédération Panafricaine des Cinéastes (FEPACI), a post from which he resigned in 1977 to concentrate on film-making.

Filmography

1965	Et la neige n'était plus / And There Was No More Snow
1968	La terre et le paysan / The Land and the Peasant
1971	Kodou *[Wolof]*
1981	Jom, ou l'histoire d'un peuple / Jom, or The Story of a People

SANKARA, Georges   Burkina Faso

15.2.1962 Abidjan, Ivory Coast. His first film was entered for competition at the 10th Festival Panafricain du Cinéma de Ouagadougou (FESPACO) in 1986.

Filmography

1986	Anpe mon amour / Anpe My Love

SANON, Emmanuel Kalifa   Burkina Faso

1949 Bobo Dioulasso, Burkina Faso. He studied cinema at the Institut Africain d'Education Cinématographique (INAFEC) in Ouagadougou and then completed his studies at the Université de Paris (Panthéon-Sorbonne). On his return to Burkina Faso, Sanon participated in the production of television films and numerous short documentaries with the Film Production Board. In 1985 at the time of the 9th Festival Panafricain du Cinéma de Ouagadougou (FESPACO), Sanon was elected general treasurer of the Fédération Panafricaine des Cinéastes (FEPACI).

Filmography

1985	Dooba, l'héritage perdu / Dooba, the Lost Heritage
	IXème FESPACO / 9th FESPACO
1987	Desebagato *[Bambana]* / Le dernier salaire / The Last Salary
1988	La cire perdue / Wax Moulding

SANOU, Kollo Daniel   Burkina Faso

23.12.1949 Borodougou, Burkina Faso. He completed secondary schooling in Burkina Faso. He then studied at the Institut National des Arts d'Abidjan in the Ivory Coast, and at the Conservatoire Libre du Cinéma Français (CLCF) and the Institut National de l'Audiovisuel (INA), both in Paris. On his return to Burkina Faso, he became head of publicity at the Ministry of Information and Culture. His second film *Beogo Naba* (1978) won the Cultural Co-operation Prize at the 6th Festival Panafricain du Cinéma de Ouagadougou (FESPACO) in 1979.

Filmography

1977	Touyan tigui
1978	Beogo Naba *[Bambana]*
1980	Les dodos / The Dodos
1982	Pawéogo / L'émigrant / The Emigrant
1984	L'artisanat et son pays / The Craftsman and His Country
	L'aigle et le caméléon / The Eagle and the Chameleon
	Jubilé d'une cathédrale / Jubilee of a Cathedral
1987	Sarraounia
1989	FESPACO 89
1991	Jigi / Hope

See also: 75b.

1960 Cape Town, South Africa. He studied film and audio visuals at the University of Cape Town. During his studies he co-founded and helped run 'Scratch', a multi-racial nightclub specialising in black music, until it was closed down by the police. At university he made several short films on video and Super 8; after graduating (1983) he trained as a cameraman in Johannesburg. Schmitz then joined the Film Co-op, an independent film collective and participated in making *The Grabber*, a short, low-budget film depicting a gangster in Soweto and featuring Thomas Mogotlane. The pair started developing the idea for *Mapantsula*. Schmitz then worked in television as an assistant editor on documentaries and magazine programmes, as a sound editor and then as editor of the documentary *The Two Rivers* (Mark Newman, 1986). He moved to West Germany and edited television documentaries at WDR Fernsehen (1985-87). Encouraged by producer Max Montocchio in London, Schmitz returned to South Africa to develop the anti-government feature *Mapantsula* (1988) with Mogotlane. He has also directed documentaries on the South African political activist and poet Mzwakhe Mbuli (1989) and on COSATU, the largest trade union federation in South Africa (1991). His other films have been short video news reports and factual magazine pieces for television.

Filmography

1988	Mapantsula *[Xhosa]*
	The Twilight Zone
1989	Made in South Africa
	Mzwakhe Mbuli: The People's Poet
1990	Fruits of Defiance
1991	Hlanganani: A Short History of COSATU

SECK, Alioune Badara   Senegal

Also known as Pape B Seck. 1949 Dakar, Senegal. Seck received his film training at the Institut des Hautes Etudes Cinématographiques (IDHEC) in Paris. He is best known in Europe for his first feature film *Afrique sur Rhin / Africa on the Rhine*, which was made in Germany in 1984.

Filmography

1980	Intérieur Gare de Lyon / Gare de Lyon Interior
1983	L'île de Gorée / The Island of Gorée
1984	Afrique sur Rhin / Africa on the Rhine

SEDDIKI, Tayyeb   Morocco

1937 Essaouira, Morocco. Seddiki ran the Casablanca Theatre for thirteen years and is well-known in theatrical circles in Morocco and France. He has directed several television dramas as well as documentaries for Moroccan national television.

Filmography

1984   Zift / Concrete

SEFRAOUI, Najib   Morocco

1948 Fez, Morocco. He went to Paris and studied archaeology, art and film. Sefraoui
worked for many years on numerous documentaries and finally made his feature film début
in 1985.

Filmography

1985   Chams / Sun

SEKOUMAR, Barry   Guinea

1935 Forécariah, south-western Guinea. Sekoumar studied cinema in Belgrade and Paris.
His first passion was documentary film-making.

Filmography

1964   Koundara
        An II du 22 novembre / Year II of the 22 November Revolution
1965   L'assainissement / The Reorganisation
1966   Mory le Crabé
1969   Et vint la liberté / And Freedom Came
1972   Kampala 72
1973   Festival 73

19.11.1913 Cairo, Egypt; died Cairo 2.4.1945. His father was a merchant. After completing secondary schooling, Selim decided to become an actor and aged sixteen played his first role in the film *Taht dou al-Kamar / Under the Moonlight* (Shoukri Madi, 1929). Soon afterwards he travelled to Paris to study but returned to Cairo after only a short stay (1935). A few years later he made his directorial début and was then employed at Studio Misr as a scriptwriter; among his writing credits is the successful *Al-Ductur / The Doctor* (Niazi Mustapha, 1939). His next film as a director, *Al-Azima / The Will* (1939), is a landmark in the development of Egyptian cinema and considered its first "realist" film. Selim died during the shooting of his tenth feature film.

Filmography

1938	Wara'a al-Sitar / Behind the Curtain
1939	Al-Azima / The Will / *aka* Determination
1940	Il'al abad / Until Eternity / *aka* Forever
1942	Ahlam al-Shabab / Dreams of Youth
1943	Al-Bu'asa / Les misérables
	Qadiyyat al-Yom / The Question of Today / *aka* Today's Case
1944	Shuhuda al-Gharam / Martyrs of Love / *aka* Romeo and Juliet
	Hanan / Tenderness
1945	Al-Mazaher / The Apparitions
	Leilat al-Gomaa / Friday Night

See also: 5b.

8.1.1923 Ziguinchor, southern Senegal. His parents divorced when he was very young and he spent his childhood years divided between his father, his grandmother and several relatives in other regions. At the age of twelve he was sent to a French school in Dakar. Two years later he abandoned his studies and began to earn his living as a car mechanic, carpenter and fisherman. Sembene spent most of his spare time attending performances by local amateur theatre troupes and griots (African oral historians and traditional storytellers), as well as attending several evening classes. At the outbreak of World War II he was drafted into the French army and fought in Europe and Africa (1942-46). After his discharge he took part in the Dakar-Niger railroad strike (October 1947-March 1948), an experience which later inspired him to write the book *Les bouts de bois de Dieu / God's Bits of Wood* (1960). In 1948 Sembene went to France as a stowaway on a ship and was employed in a Citroën car factory near Paris. After three months he moved to Marseille where he began intense political and trade union activities and was nominated secretary general of the Association des Travailleurs Sénégalais en France, a Senegalese workers' union of which he was a founder member. He was also a member of the Confédération Générale des Travailleurs (CGT), a union affiliated to the Communist Party. In 1956 his first book *Le docker noir / The Black Docker* was published. The book recounts his years in Marseille and was followed by several others. However, Sembene began to realise the greater potential of cinema as a more effective method of communication for the largely illiterate mass audience. He went to Moscow to study cinema under Mark Donskoj at the Gorky Film Studio (1962). The following year he returned to Senegal to shoot his first short film, the unreleased documentary *L'empire Songhaï / The Songhaï Empire*. His next film, *Borom Sarret*, was hailed as the first professionally made African film and its success paved the way for the development of the fiction film in the mainly French-speaking parts of Africa. Sembene has written several other books and, as one of Africa's most prominent film-makers, is himself the subject of many books and articles. He founded a Wolof magazine *Kaddu* (1972) and formed his own production company, Domirev Films.

Filmography

1963	L'empire Songhaï / The Songhaï Empire
	Borom Sarret / Le charretier
1964	Niaye *[Wolof]*
1966	La noire de ... / Black Girl
1968	Mandabi *[Wolof]* / Le mandat / The Money Order
1970	Tauw *[Wolof]* / Taaw
1971	Emitaï *[Dyola]* / Dieu du tonnerre / God of Thunder
1974	Xala *[Wolof]* / L'impuissance temporaire / The Curse
1976	Ceddo *[Wolof]*
1988	Camp de Thiaroye / Camp Thiaroye (co-dir **Thierno Faty Sow**)

See also: 22/Ib, 25/IIb, 30b, 51/Ib, 135/If, 147b.

SENE ABSA, Mousa   Senegal

1958 Dakar, Senegal. He received his primary and secondary education in Dakar. Sene Absa worked as a stage actor, mainly with the Théâtre en Spirale de Dakar (1985-86). He took a course in cinematography at the Université de Paris VIII. He has acted in several films, including *Espionne et tais-tois / Shut Up and Keep Spying* by the French film-maker Claude Boissol.

Filmography

1988   Le prix du mensonge / The Price of Lies
1990   Ken Bugul *[Wolof]* / La république des enfants / The Children's Republic

SESSOUMA, Yossala Bamoussa   Burkina Faso

22.5.1956 N'Dorola, Burkina Faso. After studying modern literature at the Université de Ouagadougou, he enrolled at the Institut Africain d'Education Cinématographique (INAFEC). After graduation he began working as an assistant director and sound engineer on several films. His début film is a documentary on the 9th Festival Panafricain du Cinéma de Ouagadougou (FESPACO) in 1985.

Filmography

1985   Reportage sur le IXème FESPACO / Report on the 9th FESPACO

SHEWA, Moise   Cameroon

9.4.1959 Kumba, Cameroon. Shewa enrolled at the Université de Yaoundé where he studied English and African literature. After graduation (1985) he spent a year teaching at a primary school. He was awarded a scholarship by the Cameroonian government to study abroad. Shewa came to England and enrolled at the London International Film School (grad. 1987). He has worked as a production manager for the Central Office of Information in London.

Filmography

1987   The Broken Pot (unreleased)

SIBITA, Arthur   Cameroon

17.6.1948 San Melima, Cameroon. He studied modern theatre and literature. He is a trained teacher and was the editor of the Cameroonian Film Board's publication *The World of Cinema*. A self-taught film-maker, Sibita made his début film *Le chef est mort: vive le chef / The Chief Is Dead: Long Live the Chief* in 1974.

Filmography

1974   Le chef est mort: vive le chef / The Chief Is Dead: Long Live the Chief
        Les enfants de l'écran / Children of the Screen
1978   Semaine culturelle du 20 mai 1978 / Cultural Week of the 20th May 1978
        La voix du poète au Mont Cameroun / The Voice of a Poet on Mount
           Cameroon
        Maîtres et disciples / Master and Disciples
1979   La guitare brisée / The Broken Guitar
1981   No Time To Say Goodbye
1983   Les coopérants / The Co-operators

SIMÃO, Luis Manuel Martino   Mozambique

20.10.1955 Nampula province, northern Mozambique. After the independence of his country from Portugal (1975), he became involved in the creation of the Instituto Nacional de Cinema (INC) in Maputo and later became its director general (1983). Simao began his professional career as an assistant cameraman and worked as director of photography with fellow Mozambican film-maker **Cardoso** on his film *Canta meu irmão, ajuda-me a cantar / Sing, Brother, Help Me To Sing* (1982). All his films have been documentaries.

Filmography

1976	Visita do presidente Kaunda / President Kaunda's Visit
	Pafure e mavue
1977	Conferência africana de cinema / African Cinema Conference
1978	Comunicado presidencial / Presidential Speech
	Estas são as armas / These Are the Weapons (co-dir Murilo Salles)
1980	Pela libertação da África austral / For the Liberation of Southern Africa
1981	Angoche, tradição e pesca / Angoche, Tradition and Fishing
	Unidade em festa / Party at the Unit
1982	Chitembene
	70 anos de kim il sung
1983	8 dias com a polisario
	Um inimigo comum / A Mutual Enemy
1986	África na Suécia / Africa in Sweden (co-dir **Martin Mhando**)

See also: 100/IIf.

SISSAKO, Abderrahmane   Mauritania

October 1961 Kiffa, Assaba region, Mauritania. His father is Malian and his mother Mauritanian. Sissako spent his early childhood in Mali before going to Mauritania in 1980. He studied literature at university but decided to express himself better through film. He was awarded a scholarship to study cinema at VGIK in Moscow and made his début in 1991.

Filmography

1991	Le jeu / The Game

SISSOKO, Cheikh Oumar   Mali

1955 San, a heavily populated quarter of Bamako, Mali. He graduated in African history and sociology from university in Paris and then took a diploma in direction, montage and cinematography at the Ecole Nationale Louis Lumière. He returned to Mali and became an official of the Centre National de Production Cinématographique (CNPC) in Bamako, for which he accomplished several short-length films, including *Sécheresse et exode rural / Drought and Rural Depopulation* (1984).

Filmography

1984	Sécheresse et exode rural / Drought and Rural Depopulation
1986	Nyamanton *[Bambana]* / La leçon des ordures / Lessons from the Garbage
1989	Finzan *[Bambana]*

See also: 53/Ib, 60/IIb.

SMIHI, Moumen   Morocco

1945 Tangier, Morocco. After completing his higher education at the Université Mohammed V in Rabat, he gained his film training at the Institut des Hautes Etudes Cinématographiques (IDHEC) in Paris. In Paris he also attended seminars led by Roland Barthes at the Practical School of Advanced Studies in Semiology.

Filmography

1975	Al-Chergui
1982	Quarante-quatre, ou les récits de la nuit / Forty-Four, or Bedtime Stories
1988	Quftan al-Hubb / Caftan of Love

SOKHONA, Sidney   Mauritania

1952 Tachott, Mauritania. He received his primary education in Tachott. In 1967 he left Mauritania to go to Paris where he worked during the day and studied in the evenings. In 1970 he enrolled at the Université de Paris VIII to study film.

Filmography

1970	Orphelins de dieu / Orphans of God
1975	Nationalité: immigré / Nationality: Immigrant
1978	Safrana ou le droit à la parole / Safrana or Freedom of Speech

SOU, Jacob   Burkina Faso

3.5.1948 Diébougou, western Burkina Faso. He trained in theatre, journalism and cinema. He has acted on the stage and worked as a reporter for national radio in Burkina Faso. Sou was director of the Centre Regional d'Action Culturelle in Lomé, Togo and has also worked for the Société Africaine de Production Cinématographique (CINAFRIC) in Ouagadougou. Both his films to date are features.

Filmography

1987	Histoire d'Orokia / Horokia's Story (co-dir Jacques Oppenheim)
1989	Le grotto / The Grotto

SOUDANI, Mohamed   Algeria

1949 El Asnam, Algeria. He studied at the Institut des Hautes Etudes Cinématographiques (IDHEC) in Paris. After graduation Soudani worked as a cameraman for Algerian television (1970-71). From 1972 he lived in Switzerland where he worked in the Polivideo production company in Locarno, firstly as a cameraman and subsequently as a director of photography (1982-87). He is currently a freelance director and producer of photography. He has also run various courses for cameramen and lighting specialists on behalf of several television companies.

Filmography

1988   Nawa / Acqua
1989   YIRIBAKRO / Bosco Sacro

SOUMANO, Amadou   Niger

1954 Goudel, Niger. He trained as sound engineer in West Germany. In 1980 he co-directed a medium-length feature *On dit africain pour ne pas nous vexer / They Call Us African To Spare Our Feelings*.

Filmography

1980   On dit africain pour ne pas nous vexer / They Call Us African To Spare
        Our Feelings (co-dir Anna Söhring)
1981   L'aide allemande vue par un œil africain / German Aid Seen Through
        African Eyes

1953 Lourenço Marques (now Maputo), Mozambique. He trained as a photojournalist. Souza left Mozambique clandestinely (1972) to join FRELIMO (Front for the Liberation of Mozambique) during the liberation war against the Portuguese and was responsible for the propagation of information. He became manager-producer at the Instituto Nacional de Cinema in Maputo (1987-88). Souza has also worked on other films as an editor, such as *Limpopo Line* (**Bright**, 1989) or as assistant director, most notably on the Mozambican/Yugoslav co-production *O tempo dos leopardos / Vreme leoparda / Time of the Leopards* (Zdravko Velimirović, 1985).

Filmography

1980	Ofensiva / Offensive
	Cinco tiros de mauser / Five Mauser Shots (co-dir **João Manuel Abranches Martins Costa**)
1981	Operação leopardo / Operation Leopard
1982	Ibo, o sangue do silêncio / Ibo, the Blood of Silence (co-dir **João Manuel Abranches Martins Costa**)
	Cinco vezes mais / Five More Times (co-dir **João Manuel Abranches Martins Costa**)
1983	Agressão... um dia 7.21 H / Aggression One Day 07.21 Hours
	Porque alguma voz são todas as vozes / Why Are Some Voices All Voices? (co-dir **João Manuel Abranches Martins Costa**)
1984	Acordo de Nkomati / The Nkomati Accord (co-dir **João Manuel Abranches Martins Costa**)
	Gorongoza
1987	Não mataram o sonho de patrício / They Did Not Destroy Patricio's Dream (co-dir **Ismaël Marcelino Vuvo**)
1990	Severino

See also: 47/IIf, 149/If.

SOW, Thierno Faty   Senegal

23.12.1941 Thiès, Senegal. After studying at the Conservatoire Libre du Cinéma Français in Paris, he worked as an assistant director for French radio and television (1964-69). Sow returned to Senegal to work as a director for Senegalese television (1969-74). He was a founder member of CINESEAS, the Association of Senegalese Film-Makers and the Fédération Panafricaine des Cinéastes (FEPACI).

Filmography

1970	La journée de Djibril N'Diaye / Djibril N'Diaye's Day (co-dir Pierre Blanchard, Pap Sow, Pap Thiam)
	Guereo, village de Djibril N'Diaye / Guereo, Village of Djibril N'Diaye
1974	L'option / The Option
1977	Feux de brousse / Bush Fires
	Exode rural / Rural Depopulation
	Education sanitaire / Sanitary Education
	Sunu koppe
1981	L'œil / The Eye
1988	Camp de Thiaroye / Camp Thiaroye (co-dir **Ousmane Sembene**)

See also: 25/IIb, 127f.

TAKAM, Jules   Cameroon

1947 Yaoundé, Cameroon. He took a course in editing at the Conservatoire Libre du Cinéma Français in Paris. He worked as an editor for a while before directing his first film in 1972.

Filmography

1972	L'attente / The Wait
1981	L'appât du gain / The Lure of Profit

TAOKO, Augustin Roch   Burkina Faso

1947 Koudougou, Burkina Faso. After leaving school he trained as a teacher before going to Paris where he took a course in film. On his return to Burkina Faso, he worked for national television and directed his first film in 1975.

Filmography

1975	M'ba - Raogo
1984	Buud Gombe / Tambour de fer / Iron Drum
1985	La vache de Rosay / Rosay's Cow

TAZI, Mohamed Abderrahman   Morocco

1942 Fez, Morocco. He studied film at the Institut des Hautes Etudes Cinématographiques (IDHEC) in Paris and also mass media and communication at Syracuse University in New York. Tazi has worked as a director of photography on several films and became an adviser and director of production for various foreign film directors working in Morocco, including Francis Coppola and John Huston.

Filmography

1976	Sui guaritori filippini / On the Filipino Healers
1981	Ibn al-Sabil / Le grand voyage / The Great Voyage
1987	Aux portes de l'Europe / At the Gateway of Europe
1989	Badis

TCHISSOUKOU, Jean-Michel   Congo

1942 Pointe-Noire, Congo; died 1987. Tchissoukou studied film-making in Paris, attending both the Institut National de l'Audiovisuel (INA) at Bry-sur-Marne and OCORA/Radio France. He worked as an assistant to Guadeloupean film director Sarah Maldoror on her feature *Sambizanga* (1972).

Filmography

1971	Illusions
1977	L'enfant et la famille / Child and Family
1979	La chapelle / The Chapel
1982	M'Pongo / Les lutteurs / Wrestlers

TCHUILEN, Jean-Claude   Cameroon

23.2.1955 Bajou, Cameroon. After secondary school he went to Paris where he enrolled for a course in film at the Conservatoire Libre du Cinéma Français; he also studied drama. He made his first film in 1981.

Filmography

1981	Le cri pluriel / The Cry of the Multitude
	Ma chère Alice / My Dear Alice
1983	Suicides

1954 Bafoussam, Cameroon. He holds an MA in audio visual communication from the Université de Valenciennes et du Hainaut-Cambresis in France. Since 1982 he has worked as an editor for FR3, the French television station. He has also worked as a critic for *Buana* magazine.

Filmography

1984	Schubbah
1985	Hommage / Homage
	Fièvre jaune taximan / Yellow Fever Taximan
1987	La gifle et la caresse / The Slap and the Stroke
	De Ouaga à Douala en passant par Paris / Ouaga to Douala via Paris
1988	L'eau de misère / Bikutsi Water Blues
1990	Le dernier voyage / The Last Trip
1991	Afrique je te plumerai / Africa, I'll Pluck Your Feathers

THIAM, Momar   Senegal

24.9.1929 Dakar. His family were jewellers. Thiam received his primary and secondary education in Dakar. For nine years he worked as an accountant before going to Paris to study stills photography. He gained further training at the Studios de Boulogne outside Paris. When he returned from Paris, Thiam started to work in the film department of the Ministry of Information in Senegal. He made his first film *Sarzan* (1963), from a story by Birago Diop.

Filmography

1963	Sarzan
1964	N'Dakarou *[Wolof]* (co-dir Papa Ibra Tal)
1967	La malle de Maka Kouli / Maka Kouli's Trunk
1968	Luttes casamançaises / Casamance Wrestling
1969	Simb, le jeu du faux lion / Simb, or the False Lion's Game
1971	Karim *[Wolof]*
1974	Baks *[Wolof]* / Chanvre indien / Cannabis
1982	Sa Dagga-Le M'Bandakatt *[Wolof]* / Sa Dagga-Le M'Bandakatt le troubadour / The Griot
1983	Bouki cultivateur / Bouki the Farmer

See also: 36/IIb.

THIOR, Amadou   Senegal

23.7.1951 Kaffrine, Senegal. He studied at the Ecole Nationale Louis Lumière in Paris (grad. 1983). On graduation he made *Xareek Maral / Desert Stopping-Place*, a short film which won the prize for best documentary from the EEC at the 1985 Festival Panafricain du Cinéma de Ouagadougou (FESPACO).

Filmography

1983	Xareek Maral / Desert Stopping-Place

TIENDREBEOGO, Raymond   Burkina Faso

1957 Ouagadougou, Burkina Faso.   He trained at the Institut Africain d'Education Cinématographique (INAFEC) in Ouagadougou and at the Université de Paris (Panthéon-Sorbonne). He co-directed his first film with Kabiré Sam Fidaali and it won the Jury Special Prize at the Amiens Film Festival in France.

Filmography

1986   Fal Solma / L'interpellation de l'étrange / The Heckling of the Stranger
          (co-dir Kabiré Sam Fidaali)
1988   Un boucher particulier / The Strange Butcher
1989   Emilie et Yao, enfants du soleil / Emilie and Yao, Children of the Sun

TOURE, Drissa   Burkina Faso

1952 Banfora, south-western Burkina Faso.   He received his early education in Ouagadougou and studied cinema in Paris. He made several documentaries before completing his first full-length feature film *Laada* (1991).

Filmography

1981   Le sort / Destiny
1983   Je suis productif / I'm Productive
1984   Nasabule *[Moore]*
1985   La fête pascale / The Easter Feastival (uncompleted)
1988   La ballade de la mouette / The Ballad of the Gull
1991   Laada

TOURE, Kitia   Ivory Coast

1956 Ayame, Ivory Coast. On completing his higher education, Toure went to Paris where he studied cinematography.

Filmography

1984   Comédie exotique / Exotic Comedy
1987   Maman, je veux vivre / Mama, I Want to Live

TRAORÉ, Falaba Issa   Burkina Faso

Abidjan, Ivory Coast. He studied at the Institut Africain d'Education Cinématographique (INAFEC) and at the Conservatoire Libre du Cinéma Français in Paris.

Filmography

1985   Va / Go (co-dir **Sekou Traoré**)
1989   Bilakoro *[Dyula]* (co-dir **Sekou Traoré, Dany Kouyate**)

See also: 85/IIf, 143/IIf.

TRAORÉ, Mahama Johnson   Senegal

1942 Dakar, Senegal. After secondary school he went to France and studied mechanical engineering. He also studied at the Conservatoire Libre du Cinéma Français (CLCF) in Paris where he trained as a film director (1964-66). He returned to Senegal (1968) where he worked as a programme co-ordinator for the Dakar Cinema Clubs. In the following year he shot his first film *Diankha-bi / La jeune fille / The Young Girl* with the help of some friends. In 1978 Traoré was elected secretary general of the Fédération Panafricaine des Cinéastes (FEPACI), a post from which he resigned in 1982. He then served as president of the Société Nouvelle de Production Cinématographique (SNPC), an organisation whose objective was to promote the production and exhibition of films from Senegal. All his films to date have been features.

Filmography

1969	Diankha-bi / La jeune fille / The Young Girl
	L'enfer des innocents / Hell of the Innocents / *aka* The Innocents' Hell
1970	Diegue-bi *[Wolof]* / La femme / The Young Woman
1972	Lambaaye *[Wolof]* / Truanderie / Graft
	Reou-Takh / Big City
1974	Garga M'Bosse *[Wolof]* / Cactus
1975	N'Diangane *[Wolof]* / The Koranic School Student

See also: 30b.

TRAORÉ, Mory   Ivory Coast

1951 Abidjan, Ivory Coast. He began studying law in his own country and then went to Paris where he did various jobs to maintain himself. In 1974 he enrolled at the Conservatoire National Supérieur d'Art Dramatique de Paris (CNSAD). After graduating he went to Japan where he studied various theatre forms, Shintoism, martial arts and the Japanese language. He returned to the Ivory Coast and began to direct stage plays by contemporary authors. In 1976 he directed his first film *Le comédien et son texte / The Actor and His Text* which was inspired by the story of the English King Richard I.

Filmography

1976	Le comédien et son texte / The Actor and His Text
1979	L'homme d'ailleurs / The Outsider / *aka* The Man from Elsewhere

TRAORÉ, Nissi Joanny

1952 Takaledougou, Burkina Faso. He studied in Germany and then at the Institut National de l'Audiovisuel (INA) at Bry-sur-Marne in Paris.

Filmography

1985	Paris solidarité / Paris Solidarity
1986	L'autre école / The Other School

TRAORÉ, Sekou

1962 Bobo Dioulasso, Burkina Faso. He graduated from the Institut Africain d'Education Cinématographique in Ouagadougou.

Filmography

1985	Va / Go (co-dir **Falaba Issa Traoré**)
1989	Bilakoro *[Dyula]* (co-dir **Dany Kouyate, Falaba Issa Traoré**)

See also: 85/IIf, 141/IIf.

TSAKI, Brahim   Algeria

27.12.1946 Sidi-bel-Abbès, western Algeria. Tsaki studied film at the Institut National des Arts du Spectacle et Techniques de Diffusion (INSAS) in Brussels. Both his films to date have been about the lives of children.

Filmography

1981	Abna al-Rih / Children of the Wind
1983	Hikaya liqa' / Story of an Encounter

UGBOMAH, Eddie   Nigeria

Lagos, Nigeria. Ugbomah spent his childhood in Lagos and then went to London to study journalism, drama, film and television production. He worked briefly for the BBC and played small roles in several films, including *Dr No* (Terence Young, 1962). He returned to Nigeria and decided to get involved in film production (1976). In 1977 he made his first film *The Rise and Fall of Dr Oyenusi*.

Filmography

1977	The Rise and Fall of Dr Oyenusi
1978	The Boy is Good
1979	The Mask
1981	Oil Doom
1982	Boulos 80
1983	Death of a Black President
1984	Vengeance of the Cult
1985	Esan

Guinea Bissau. U'kset has worked as a radio and television comedian and actor. In 1975 he created an orchestra, 'the West African Cosmos'.

Filmography

1986   N'tturudu / The Mask

UYS, Jamie   South Africa

Full name: Jacobus Johannes Uys. 1921 Boksburg, Transvaal, South Africa. He was initially employed as a mine-worker. After studying at the University of Pretoria, Uys became a teacher at a school near Johannesburg. He then married and moved to his father-in-law's ranch near the Palala River in the northern Transvaal; he then worked as a rancher for three years and developed his love of nature and wildlife. Fascinated by the possibilities of making a film against the background of the bush, Uys turned to film-making. His début film, the comedy *Daar doer in die bosveld / Far Away in the Bushveld* (1951), was produced, written, directed, shot and edited by Uys; the only roles were taken by him and his wife. Most of his subsequent films, made with small crews and low budgets, have been international box-office successes, particularly the two popular *The Gods Must Be Crazy* films. He has also made several documentaries for the State Information Services. His production company, Jamie Uys Films, has produced several films, including *Satanskoraal / Satanscoral* (Elmo de Witt, 1959) and *Rip van Wyk* (Emil Nofal, 1960). His only film made outside South Africa is *All the Way to Paris*, produced in France in 1966.

Filmography

1951	Daar doer in die bosveld / Far Away in the Bushveld
1952	Vyftig-vyftig / Fifty-Fifty
1953	Daar doer in die stad / Far Away in the City
1954	Geld soos bossies / Money to Burn
1958	Die bosvelder / The Bushvelder
1961	Doodkry is min / Ineradicable Is My Name
	Hans en die rooinek / Hans and the Redneck
1962	Lord Oom Piet / Lord Uncle Piet
1964	Dingaka *[Sotho]* / Doctors
1966	All the Way to Paris
1967	Professor en die Prikkelpop / The Professor and the Beauty Queen
1969	Dirkie / *aka* Lost in the Desert
1973	Beautiful People
1976	Funny People
1980	The Gods Must Be Crazy
1983	Funny People II
1991	The Gods Must Be Crazy II
1992	Adventures in Africa

VIEYRA, Paulin Soumanou   Senegal

30.1.1925 Porto Novo, Dahomey (now Benin); died 10.12.1987 Paris, France. He received his early education in Porto Novo. At the age of ten his father sent him to a boarding school in France, after which he studied biological sciences at the Université de Paris. Whilst at university Vieyra came into contact with the cinema, as an extra playing an African soldier in the film *Le diable au corps / Devil in the Flesh* (Claude Autant-Lara, 1946). In 1952 he enrolled at the Institut des Hautes Etudes Cinématographiques (IDHEC), also in Paris (grad. 1954). During his studies he made a short film *C'était il y a quatre ans / Four Years Ago* (1954). He also worked for several French directors as an assistant, including André Berthomieu on *Quatre jours à Paris / Four Days in Paris* (1955). In the following year Vieyra shot his first professional film with a group of friends, *Afrique sur Seine / Africa on the Seine*. He also worked as an editor for Canadian television. Returning to Senegal, Vieyra joined the Ministry of Information as head of the film division. During this period he helped to record many of the historical events taking place as many African countries were gaining their independence. After retiring from the Ministry of Information, Vieyra devoted most of his time to writing books and articles and lecturing on African cinema throughout Africa, Europe and the United States. Among his books are *Le cinéma et l'Afrique / The Cinema and Africa* (1969), *Ousmane Sembene cinéaste* (1972) and *Le cinéma au Sénégal / The Cinema in Senegal* (1983). He was treasurer of the Fédération Panafricaine des Cinéastes (FEPACI) (1970-75). Vieyra worked as a documentary film-maker in Senegal for nearly thirty years and among his few feature films is *En résidence surveillée / Under House Arrest* (1981). *L'envers du décor / The Other Side of the Decoration* (1981) is a documentary on fellow Senegalese director **Sembene**.

Filmography

1954	C'était il y a quatre ans / Four Years Ago
1955	Afrique sur Seine / Africa on the Seine (co-dir Mamadou Sarr)
1957	L'Afrique à Moscou / Africa in Moscow
1958	Le Niger aujourd'hui / Niger Today
1959	Les présidents Senghor et Modibo Keita / Presidents Senghor and Modibo Keita
	Avec les africains à Vienne / Africans in Vienna
	Présence africaine à Rome / The African Presence in Rome
1960	Indépendance du Cameroun, Togo, Congo et Madagascar / The Independence of Cameroon, Togo, Congo and Madagascar
1961	Une nation est née / A Nation Is Born
1963	Lamb / Senegalase Wrestling
1964	Ecrit au Caire / Written in Cairo / *aka* A Letter from Cairo
1965	N'Diangane *[Wolof]*
	Sindiély *[Wolof]*
1966	Mol / Un homme un idéal une vie / *aka* Les pêcheurs / Fishermen (begun 1957)
	Le Sénégal au festival mondial des arts nègres / Senegal in the World Festival of Black Arts

1967	La bicyclette/le gâteau/au marché/rendez-vous / *aka* Spécial Sénégal / The bicycle/the cake/at the market/meeting
1974	Ecrits de Dakar / Letters from Dakar
	Diarama / Welcome
	L'art plastique / Plastic Arts
1976	L'habitat urbain au Sénégal / Urban Housing in Senegal
	L'habitat rural au Sénégal / Rural Housing in Senegal
1981	Birago Diop, conteur / Birago Diop, Storyteller
	L'envers du décor / Behind the Scenes (begun 1976)
	En résidence surveillée / Under House Arrest
1983	Iba N'Diaye, peintre / Iba N'Diaye, Painter

See also: 70b.

VUVO, Ismaël Marcelino

Mozambique

10.6.1959 Chibuto, Mozambique. He received his primary and secondary education in Maputo. In 1977 he enrolled for a nine-month editing course at the Instituto Nacional de Cinema (INC), Mozambique's national film institute. He gained experience as an editor on several films before making his directorial début in 1979.

Filmography

1979	Assim elas vivem / Such Is Their Life (co-dir **Josué Mutelo Chabela, Enoque Maté**)
1981	Alcoolismo o que e? / What Does Alcoholism Mean?
1982	Queimadas / Burning (co-dir José Baptista)
1983	Hora de construir / Time To Build
1987	Não mataram o sonho de patrício / They Did Not Destroy Patricio's Dream (co-dir **Camillo de Souza**)

See also: 43f, 134f.

WADE, Mansour Sora

Senegal

1949 Dakar, Senegal. He completed his primary and secondary education in Dakar. He then went to Paris (1973) and took courses in cinematography and audio visual studies at the Université de Paris (grad. 1976). Wade is a founder member of several theatre companies, including the AGIT-ART in Dakar. He is also a member of the Société des Réalisateurs Sénégalais, the association of Senegalese film-makers.

Filmography

1976	Lambju mag II
	L'avare et l'étranger / The Miser and the Stranger
	Bi Beggel
1983	Contrastes / Contrasts
1989	Fary l'ânesse / Fary the She-Ass
1990	Taal Pex

1955 Kisumu, Nyanza province, north-western Kenya. He graduated from the University of Nairobi with an honours degree (1979). Wandago worked as a playwright and theatre director and as a journalist for *The Weekly Review* before enrolling at the Kenya Institute of Mass Communication (KIMC) in Nairobi, from where he graduated with a diploma in film production (1981) and where later he lectured (1986-90). He has taken part in many stage, television and theatre productions. He now owns his own company Alwan Communications, based in Nairobi.

Filmography

1982	The White Veil
1984	Feeding the Nation

YALA, Mohamed Ameziane   Algeria

16.9.1946 Akfadou, Algeria. He studied cinema at Łódź Film School in Poland. On graduation he went to Rome where he worked briefly in television and as a film critic. Since 1971 Yala has directed many short documentary films.

Filmography

1971	Fantazia
1973	Lettre de Tizi-Ouzou / Letter from Tizi-Ouzou
	Les aurès aujourd'hui / The Aurès Today
	Oasis - terre nouvelle / Oasis - Young Land
1974	L'oléiculture / Olive Cultivation
	La céréaliculture / Cereal Growing
1975	Bataille de la production / Production Battle
	Jeux méditerranéens / Mediterranean Games
	Par le peuple et pour le peuple / By the People for the People
1976	Je parviendrai / I Will Succeed
	La constitution / The Constitution
1977	Rétine comme regard / Retinal Glance
1980	Crépuscule / Twilight
1981	Balad El Baroud / Country of Gun Powder
	Eternel novembre / Eternal November
1983	Chant d'automne / Autumn Song / *aka* Songs of Autumn

15.5.1955 Koudougou, Burkina Faso. He completed his secondary schooling in Koudougou and in the Ivory Coast. In 1979 he went to Paris where he studied photography at the Ecole Française d'Enseignement Technique (EFET). He also studied at the Conservatoire Libre du Cinéma Français (CLCF) (1980-83) and then transferred to the Université de Paris VIII where he received a degree in communication studies. He returned to Burkina Faso where he qualified as an editor at the national television station. He edited **Zoumbara**'s film *Jours de tourmente / Days of Torment* (1983). Yameogo also worked as assistant technician on several films by **Idrissa Ouedraogo**. All his films have been features.

Filmography

1984   L'œuf silhouette / The Silhouetted Egg
1987   Dunia *[Moore]* / Le monde / The World
1990   Laafi *[Moore]* / Tout va bien / All Is Well

YARNEY, Aato　　　　　　　　　　　　　　　　　　　Ghana

22.1.1932 Senya Beraku, southern Ghana. Yarney received his early education in Accra. He enrolled at the London International Film School to study film (1961) and graduated a year later with a diploma in film technique. He also attended extra-mural courses organised jointly by the British Film Institute and the University of London. Yarney then went to Poland to study film direction (1965-66). He has worked as a production assistant, scriptwriter, producer and head of production for the Ghana Film Industry Corporation. His cousin is the film-maker **Kwaw Paintsil Ansah**.

Filmography *(dates unknown)*

Panoply of Ghana
Market Day
Golden Pod
Population Census
Cult of Twins
The New Breed
Rainbow Colours
His Majesty's Sergeant

See also: 18/IIb.

YASHFIN, Ahmed　　　　　　　　　　　　　　　　　Morocco

Morocco. Yashfin studied cinema in Los Angeles. On his return to Morocco, he was involved in several documentary productions before directing his first film in 1984.

Filmography

1984　　Al-Kaboos / The Nightmare

See also: 11/IIb.

YEO, Kozoloa   Ivory Coast

1950 Tioro, Chad. After completing his secondary education, Yeo went to France where he enrolled at the Ecole Nationale Louis Lumière in Paris to study cinematography. Together with fellow Ivory Coast film-maker **Koula** he formed a production company, Les Films de la Montagne (1978). They have worked together on several publicity films.

Filmography

1976	Espoir / Hope
1980	La Côte d'Ivoire et la mer / Ivory Coast and the Sea (co-dir **Jean-Louis Koula**)
	Les métiers du bâtiment / Building Crafts (co-dir **Jean-Louis Koula**)
1983	Pétanqui / Le droit à la vie / The Right to Life

See also: 84/IIf.

YONLY, René-Bernard   Burkina Faso

1945 Tansarga, Burkina Faso. He received his primary education at the Catholic mission of Diapaga and completed his secondary schooling at Fada N'Gourma in western Burkina Faso. Yonly then started working as an assistant librarian at the Université de Ouagadougou. He joined the Film Club in Ouagadougou and at the same time began his film-making training.

Filmography

1973	Sur le chemin de la réconciliation / On the Path to Reconciliation

ZEMMOURI, Mahmoud   Algeria

22.12.1946 Boufarik, northern Algeria. He studied cinema at the Institut des Hautes Etudes Cinématographiques (IDHEC) in Paris. Zemmouri has directed the majority of his films in France.

Filmography

1981	Prends dix mille balles et casses-toi / Take 1000 Quid and Shove Off
1983	Les folles années du twist / The Crazy Years of the Twist
1990	De Hollywood à Tamanrasset / From Hollywood To Tamanrasset

ZIYANE, Nkosingphile   Swaziland

30.4.1956 Manzini, Swaziland. Ziyane began his schooling at the St Philomena primary school in Manzini (1962); in 1969 he attended the Salesian High School, also in Manzini. After leaving school he worked as a photographer for the Swaziland National Museum in Lobamba and the Cineclub Vrijheidsfilms, a Tanzanian-based Dutch company (1974-76). He later enrolled at the Tanzanian School of Journalism (1981-84). In 1984 Ziyane left for Ghana in order to pursue his studies in film at the National Film and Television Institute. After graduating (1987) he returned to work for the Cineclub Vrijheidsfilms (until 1990). He is currently working as a journalist for *The Times* of Swaziland. His second film is an account of the black American editor and writer William Edward Burghardt Dubois (1868-1963).

Filmography

1985	Children in Exile
	The Re-Internment of Dr W E B Dubois
1986	Africa Responds to the World
1987	The Family Next Door
1988	Ruvu-Masuguru, a Refugee Camp

ZOUMBARA, Paul   Burkina Faso

5.4.1949 Souanké, Congo. He received his early education in Souanké and studied literature at the Université de Ouagadougou in Burkina Faso. After graduation he went to France where he enrolled at a film school in Paris. On his return home he joined the Burkina Faso Film Board (1977). He worked as an assistant director before becoming involved in film production in Ouagadougou. He directed his first film *Le pape à Ouagadougou / The Pope in Ouagadougou* in 1980.

Filmography

1980	Le pape à Ouagadougou / The Pope in Ouagadougou
1981	Cauchemar / Nightmare
1983	Jours de tourmente / Days of Torment

See also: 152b.

ZRAN, Mohamed   Tunisia

23.8.1959 Zarzis, south-eastern Tunisia. He studied cinematography in Paris and in 1987 released his first film *Virgule / Comma*. His most recent film was presented at the 1990 Cannes Film Festival.

Filmography

1987	Virgule / Comma
1989	Le casseur de pierres / The Stone Breaker

Film Title Index

Film Title Index

This index includes all film titles, including original language titles and foreign language, English language and *aka* versions. It has been compiled in a word-by-word alphabetical order, for which purpose all definite and indefinite articles in all languages, together with accents and other diacritical marks, brackets, commas, question marks and exclamation marks have been ignored. These definite and indefinite articles are as follows: die, 'n (Afrikaans); al-, el- (Arabic); a, an, the (English); l' la, le, les, un, une (French); a, as, o, os, um, uma, umas, uns (Portuguese). Apostrophised words are arranged such that, for example, the film *A Child's Tears* appears after all titles beginning with *Child*. Hyphenated words and initials are treated as two words. Abbreviations are treated as one word; the English abbreviations Dr, Mr, Mrs, No. and St are listed as if they were spelt out in full. Identical titles are dated and listed chronologically, unless they are of the same date, in which case either the country or director is indicated. Film titles containing a number are listed together with its equivalent in words in brackets: for example, *[trois] 3 ans 5 mois* and *[three] 3 Years 5 Months*.

G

Gabon, a Country of Contrasts *see* Gabon, pays de
   contraste   59/lf
Gabon, pays de contraste   59/lf
Gafiré's Doctor *see* Le médecin de Gafiré
         25/llb, 57/lf
Game, The *see* Le jeu   130/llf
Gandji's Death *see* La mort de Gandji   15b, 15f
Ganga   111/llf
Ganvié mon village   3/llf
Ganvié My Village *see* Ganvié mon village   3/llf
Gap in the Wall, The *see* La brèche dans le mur
         64/llb, 64/llf
gardienne des champs, La *see* Koligure   98/llf
Gare de Lyon Interior *see* Intérieur Gare de Lyon
         124/lf
Garga M'Bosse   142/lf
Gary al-Wuhush   1f
Gawab   24f
Gboundo   69/llf
Geld soos bossies   146f
Geliefde land   119f
Geluksdal   117f
General View of the Professional Centre of
   N'Kembo *see* Vue générale du centre
   professionnel de N'Kembo   85/lf
Generation 50 *see* Geração 50   42f
Genesis Chapter X   118/llf
Gentle Johnny *see* Sagmoedige neelsie   117f
Gentlemen, The *see* Al-Sada al-Rijal   12/llf
Geração 50   42f
German Aid Seen Through African Eyes *see* L'aide
   allemande vue par un œil africain   133/llf
geste de Ségou, La *see* Segu-Janjo   48/llf
Get Up! *see* Yiki-Yan   109b, 109f
Geti Tey   104f
Gharib, Al-   13f
Ghariba   24f
Ghira al-Katila, Al-   14f
Ghoroub wa Shorouk   13f
Ghost Stories *see* Spookstories   37/llf
Giant in the Sun   73f
gifle et la caresse, La   138f
Gil el Gadid, Al-   24f
Gilded Chair of Tutankhamen, The *see* Korsi Tout
   Ankh Amoun al Zahaby   2/lf
Girl, The *see* Den muso   46f
Girls and the Summer, The *see* El Banat wal sayf 6f
Give and Take *see* Du donner et du reçevoir   40/llf
Give Me Back My Father *see* Rendez-moi mon père
         55f
Give Me Shelter   17b
Gnaouas   68/llf
Go *see* Va   141/llf, 143/llf
God Is Great *see* Allah Akbar   6f
God Is With Us *see* Allah ma'na   24f
God of Thunder *see* Emitaï   127f
God's Gift *see* Wend Kuuni   78f
God's Will *see* Allah Tantou   7/lf
Gods and the Dead, The *see* Os deuses e os mortos
         72/llf
Gods Must Be Crazy, The   146b, 146f
Gods Must Be Crazy II, The   146b, 146f
Gold Leaf *see* Safaih min dhahab   39/llf

Gold - The Traditional Lost Wax Process   105/lf
Golden Hooves *see* Safaih min dhahab   39/llf
Golden Pod   153/lf
Golden Sands *see* Rimal min dhahab   44f
Goob na nu   63/llf
Good News   117f
Goodbye To Your Love *see* Wadda' tu hubbak   44f
Gorongoza   134f
Gouyoush al chams   2/lf, 14b
Governor General of Chakerbakerben Island, The
   see Al-Hakem al-'am   88/lf
Grabber, The   123b
Graft *see* Lambaaye   142/lf
grand combat pour l'autosuffisance alimentaire, Le
         26/lf
grand voyage, Le *see* Ibn al-Sabil   136/llf
grande case Bamiléké, La   106/lf
grande date, La   79/llf
Grandmother *see* Yaaba   110f
Grass Is Singing, The   114/llf
grasse matinée, La   99/llf
Great Battle for Alimentary Self-Sufficiency, The
   see Le grand combat pour l'autosuffisance
   alimentaire   26/lf
Great Clown, The *see* Al-Muharrij al-Kabir   44f
Great Fairs of Upper Volta, The *see* Foires générales
   voltaïques   111/llb
Great Voyage, The *see* Ibn al-Sabil   136/llf
Griot, The *see* Sa Dagga-Le M'Bandakatt   139/llf
grotto, Le   132/llf
Grotto, The *see* Le grotto   132/llf
Grow Beetroot *see* Cultivez la betterave   87/llf
Growing Cotton *see* Récolte du coton   61f
Guereo, village de Djibril N'Diaye   135/llf
Guereo, Village of Djibril N'Diaye *see* Guereo, village
   de Djibril N'Diaye   135/lf
guérisseurs, Les   25/llb, 25/llf
Guerre de libération   32/llf
guerre du pétrole n'aura pas lieu, La   34/llf
Guilty, The *see* Al-Modhniboon   95f
Guinean School, The *see* L'école guinéenne   40/llf
guitare brisée, La   129/llf
Guns, The *see* Os fuzis   72/llf

H

Habitat *see* L'habitat   26/lf
habitat, L'   26/lf
habitat en république populaire du Congo, L'   79/llf
habitat rural au Sénégal, L'   148f
habitat urbain au Sénégal, L'   148f
Hadda   68/lb
Hadha huwwa al-hubb   6f
Hadutha masriyya   44f
Hafia, Africa's Three Times Champion *see* Hafia,
   triple champion d'Afrique   53/llf
Hafia, triple champion d'Afrique   53/llf
Ha'imoon, Al-   82/llf
Hakem al-'am, Al-   88/llf
Half a Million *see* Nesf arnab   82/lf
Halfaouine   39/lf
Hallaq darb al-Foqara   116/llf
Hammam al-Malatili   6f
Hams *see* Chams   125/lf

Q

R

S

General Index

This index includes educational institutions, organisations, film bodies and companies, titles of books and plays, and film personalities other than those directors included as main entries.

Selected Bibliography

This bibliography includes reference publications which either have been helpful in the compilation of this book or may be pursued for further reading and research. Articles in periodicals and journals are not included. For a more extensive bibliography, the reader is guided to *Arab & African Film Making* by Lizbeth Malkmus and Roy Armes (pages 246-258) and to *Sub-Saharan African Films and Filmmakers: an annotated bibliography* by Nancy Schmidt.

African Films: the Context of Production
Edited by Angela Martin
London: British Film Institute, 1982.

Armes, Roy
Third World Film Making and the West
Berkeley: University of California Press, 1987.

L'Association des Trois Mondes
Dictionnaire du cinéma africain: tome 1
Paris: Editions Karthala, 1991.

Bachy, Victor
Le Cinéma au Gabon
Brussels: OCIC, 1986.

Bachy, Victor
Le Cinéma au Mali
Brussels: OCIC, 1982.

Bachy, Victor
Le Cinéma en Côte d'Ivoire
Brussels: OCIC, 1982.

Bachy, Victor
La Haute-Volta et le Cinéma
Brussels: OCIC, 1982.

Ballantyne, James and Andrew Roberts
Africa: A Handbook of Film and Video Resources
London: British Universities Film & Video Council, 1986.

Balogun, Françoise
Le Cinéma au Nigéria
Brussels and Paris: OCIC and Harmattan: 1984.

Binet, Jacques, Ferid Boughedir and Victor Bachy
Cinémas noirs d'Afrique
Paris: CinémAction (44), 1983.

Boughedir, Ferid
Le cinéma africain de A à Z
Brussels: OCIC, 1987.

Le cinéma sud-africain est-il tombé sur la tête?
Edited by Keyan Tomaselli
Paris: CinémAction (39), 1986.

Convents, Guido
Préhistoire du cinéma en Afrique 1897-1918: à la recherche des images oubliées
Brussels: OCIC, 1986.

Gabriel, Teshome
Third Cinema in the Third World: the Aesthetics of Liberation
Ann Arbor: UMI Research Press, 1982.

Khan, Mohamed
An Introduction to the Egyptian Cinema
London: Informatics, 1969.

Malkmus, Lizbeth and Roy Armes
Arab & African Film Making
London; Atlantic Highlands, New Jersey: Zed Books, 1991.

Ngakane, Lionel and Keith Shiri
Africa on Film
London: BBC, 1991.

Otten, Rik
Le Cinéma au Zaïre, au Rwanda et au Burundi
Brussels and Paris: OCIC and L'Harmattan, 1984.

Pfaff, Françoise
The Cinema of Ousmane Sembene
Westport: Greenwood Press, 1984.

Pfaff, Françoise
Twenty-Five Black African Film-Makers
Westport: Greenwood Press, 1988.

Schmidt, Nancy
Sub-Saharan African Films and Filmmakers: an annotated bibliography
London: Hans Zell Publishers, 1988.

Tomaselli, Keyan
The Cinema of Apartheid: Class and Race in South African Cinema
New York: Smyrna Press, 1987.

Vieyra, Paulin Soumanou
Le cinéma africain des origines à 1973
Paris: Présence Africaine, 1973.

Vieyra, Paulin Soumanou
Le Cinéma au Sénégal
Brussels and Paris: OCIC and Harmattan: 1983.

Vieyra, Paulin Soumanou
Le Cinéma et l'Afrique
Paris: Présence Africaine, 1969.

Vieyra, Paulin Soumanou
Ousmane Sembene cinéaste
Paris: Présence Africaine, 1972.

General

Dictionnaire du Cinéma
Edited by Jean-Loup Passek
Paris: Larousse, 1991.

Film Directors: A Complete Guide. Eighth Annual International Edition.
Compiled and edited by Michael Singer.
Beverly Hills, CA: Lone Eagle Publishing Co., 1990.

The International Dictionary of Films and Film-makers: volume 2 - Directors/Filmmakers
Editor: Christopher Lyon. Assistant Editor: Susan Doll.
Chicago; London: St James Press, 1984.

Katz, Ephraim
The Film Encyclopedia
New York: Thomas Y Crowell, 1979.

Further Information

Association des Trois Mondes
63 bis, rue du Cardinal Lemoine
75005 Paris
FRANCE
tel +331 43 54 78 69
fax +331 46 34 70 19

CENACI
B.P. 2193
Librevile
GABON

Centre National de Production
    Cinématographique (CNPC)
B.P. 116
Bamako
MALI
tel +223 225913

DIPROCI
01 B.P. 647
Ouagadougou 01
BURKINA FASO
tel + 226 302317

Egyptian Film Centre
Ministry of Culture
City of Arts
Pyramids Avenue
Cairo
EGYPT
tel +20 2 850968
fax +20 2 854701

FEPACI
01 B.P. 2524
Ouagadougou 01
BURKINA FASO
tel +226 310258
fax +226 311859

FESPACO
01 B.P. 2505
Ouagadougou 01
BURKINA FASO
tel +226 307538
fax +226 312509

Instituto Nacional de Cinema
C.P. 679
Maputo
MOZAMBIQUE
tel +258 1 29912

Showdata
PO Box 91792
Auckland Park 2006
SOUTH AFRICA
tel +27 11 482 1382
fax +27 11 726 1422
□ *Information and research company on
all aspects of the South African film and
television industries*